I'M OK
— U N T I L —
I'M NOT OK

Grief From A-Z

Margaret Fraser-Thibault

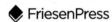 FriesenPress

Suite 300 - 990 Fort St
Victoria, BC, V8V 3K2
Canada

www.friesenpress.com

Disclaimer: All quotes are attributed where possible. I am not a certified grief counsellor, but I am well-trained and experienced in responding to grief over 45 years. It's impossible to include all aspects of grief in this book, but I offer "common" experiences from hundreds of everyday people. The names I chose are generic, with no intent to exclude any nationality or race. I use pronouns without intent to exclude anyone. Grief transcends any lines society has drawn, and I've refined it to the smallest commonality—people. We ALL hurt.

ISBN
978-1-03-911417-3 (Hardcover)
978-1-03-911416-6 (Paperback)
978-1-03-911418-0 (eBook)

1. Psychology, Grief & Loss

Distributed to the trade by The Ingram Book Company

DEDICATED TO THE LOVING MEMORY OF MY
GREATEST CHEERLEADER FOR THIS BOOK

FRANK THIBAULT

Frankie, you were my most precious hello August 17, 1974,
and my most painful goodbye April 14, 2019
There is no ending to a love story

Thank you

Thank you to my husband, Frankie, for encouraging me to write this book. He started the cheerleading at least two years prior to his death. Even from Heaven, he is still my biggest cheerleader.

Thank you to my daughter, Sheylan Thibault-Kolody, who is another cheerleader who makes me so proud every day. And thank you to her husband, Bruce Kolody, who loves her enough to share her time with me unconditionally. Thank you to our three grandsons—Bryden, Everett, and Lucas—who brought joy back into my life after Papa's death. Just thinking of them fills my heart with love and joy.

Thank you to our son Tony James, who is autistic and helped me look at his dad's death realistically and at the worst of times, reduce it to the basics: "It was an act of nature. It was not his, or anybody's, fault. He did nothing wrong." There are many ways of looking at death and grief.

Special thanks to all my family, Frank's family, and our friends and neighbors who taught me things about grief when it hits so close to home. Their encouragement led me to the finish line.

About the Author and the Book

I've had the privilege of meeting with or hearing about grieving people over fifty of my sixty-nine years. I say privilege because it was a gift when people allowed me into their lives at their most vulnerable times. They weren't asking for solutions, fixes, or magic. They were asking to be listened to, acknowledged, and validated.

I live in a small town and was blessed with fifteen years in the newspaper business: thirteen years as coordinator, advocate and provincial trainer for Victims' Services with the RCMP; eight years in the office of the Member of the Legislative Assembly; and forty-four years as a wife and mother. The joy now is that I'm Nanny to three perfect grandsons.

From my careers and life in a small town, I know there are people everywhere in painful crisis situations, and people who desperately need a phrase to hang on to, or a word of support. This book provides that.

This book is a mixture of helpful information I gained from others, print media, and social media. I searched for directions and found messages instead.

I walk beside you in your grief, as much of the information is what I experienced after the murder of four police officers I worked with in 2005, and the sudden death of my husband in early 2019.

Author's Notes

I am not a psychologist or psychiatrist, but I am a trained trauma responder, and I have over thirty years of training and experience. Thank you to Mayerthorpe Victims' Services Unit for trusting me to become your first coordinator with the RCMP, your advocate for those in trauma, and your trainer for advocates and coordinators locally and across the province. Over thirteen years, the training and information gleaned from many sources was invaluable.

Thank you deeply to the Alberta North-West Regional Victims' Services coordinators I met with once a month who shared their experiences, information and suggestions, support, and, most importantly, love. Some of their shares appear in the book.

Thank you to the RCMP in Mayerthorpe, Whitecourt, and Fox Creek detachments for their trust and support of VSU. We were honored to be called out to crisis situations with you and to learn from you while you allowed us to occasionally teach new officers about NOKs and death in small communities. Victims' Services is so much more than being the helpful face after a death, but grief is the focus of this book.

Thank you to the many strong people who shared the basis for this book. They had been through hell and back and were willing to share with me and others their shattered lives and the horror they were trying to work their minds around.

I don't want to give the impression that I did this all myself as VSU coordinator. *NOT AT ALL!* There were always trained advocates available 24/7, and they were incredible. They were volunteers who were worth all the gold in the world, and I can never thank them enough for being so giving of their hearts and time. But in this book, I speak only for me.

I learned from people who came to me over the fifteen years that I was a reporter and then editor at the local weekly newspaper, the *Freelancer*. They came to put obituaries in but stayed to talk privately about the death of their loved one. In reality, they just needed to be listened to, acknowledged, and assured that they weren't losing their minds. It was all "off the record" in those situations.

I learned from people who came into the MLA's office during my eight years there, again to ask for advice or to get help with government paperwork but staying to talk privately about the death of their loved one. They also wanted to be acknowledged and held while they cried. Again, they just needed to know they weren't going insane and they were not alone.

Bits of information came from Google and Facebook. Thank you to whoever puts the honest stuff on. Any quotes I used are attributed to the authors when they weren't listed as "unknown." Thank you, all.

Whether you're the one grieving or the one trying to understand grief better because of a friend or family member, this book contains support for you. It's probably best taken a little bit at a time.

Please know that someone cares about what you're going through.

With love and hugs, Margaret

Foreword

Grief: *"It's your road and yours alone. Others may walk it with you, but no one can walk it for you."* — *Rumi*

This book about grief is a suggested reference guideline for you. It's written to assure you that you're not alone, and you're not losing your mind. You are "grief-normal" while struggling through an extremely abnormal situation. You're holding A–Z shares in your hand from people who have walked, or are still walking with you. I have paraphrased to protect all privacy, and all names have been changed. It doesn't matter whose story it is. What matters is the message.

For grief, there is no map. No written policy and procedures. That's because each person is different, which makes your grief journey unique. But there will be places where others' journeys intersect with yours.

The words will not suit everyone and may not fit what you believe. But the information comes from many reliable sources, including the "expert sources" who have traveled the difficult path after a death. They all survived the pain and fear.

If you connect with one word, one phrase, or one story, and it helps you for a moment or a day or a week, then your momentary reprieve fills my heart with gratitude.

I have written alphabetically to show that grief runs the complete gamut from A to Z. Grief information needs to be something we can identify with quickly, as a brain can take in only small amounts of information when grieving. Thus the short stories or point form information.

I have two rules for you reading this book: 1. You must do only what feels right for *you*. 2. You must seek professional help if your grief continues to be unmanageable or if you're thinking of harming yourself or someone else. Please.

I salute every person for surviving in his or her own way. And I cheer for *you*. You're not alone. You're not losing your mind. And you will find solid ground eventually.

> "*Sometimes you have to let go of the picture of what you thought life would be like and learn to find joy in the story you're living.*" —*Rachel Marie Martin, findingjoy.net*

Index

1	A is for ADVICE
4	A is for AFTER
5	A is for AIR
6	A is for ANGELS
7	A is for ANIMALS
8	A is for ANXIETY
9	A is for ASHES
11	A is for ASSISTED DYING
14	B is for BARGAINING
15	B is for BEFORE
16	B is for BELIEF
18	B is for BLACK ARMBANDS
19	B is for BLAME
21	B is for BREAKING BREAD
22	B is for BUCKET LIST
25	C is for CANDLES
26	C is for CAREGIVERS
28	C is for CHILDREN and DEATH
31	C is for CLOSURE AFTER COURT
32	C is for COMPARATIVE GRIEF
33	C is for COURAGE
36	D is for DEFINITIONS
37	D is for DENIAL
38	D is for DIFFERENCES
40	D is for DO TELL ME ... D is for DON'T TELL ME ...
43	D is for DUTY
46	E is for EASY DEATH
46	E is for EMPTY
47	E is for EUPHEMISMS
51	F is for FEAR
52	F is for FORGIVENESS
54	F is for FRIENDS
56	F is for F***
57	F is for FUNERALS
61	G is for GOODBYE ... and GOODBYE ... and GOODBYE
63	G is for GRATITUDE
65	G is for GRIEF IS LIKE ...
67	G is for GUILT
70	H is for HEALING
71	H is for HEARTBEAT
73	H is for HEREAFTER
75	H is for HOPE
76	H is for HOW ARE YOU?
77	H is for HOW MANY CHILDREN DO YOU HAVE?
79	I is for IN BETWEEN
79	I is for INTIMACY LOST
81	I is for ISOLATION
84	J is for JEALOUSY
87	K is for KARMA
87	K is for KEEP
90	L is for LAST WORDS
91	L is for LAUGHTER

93	L is for LIFTING YOUR SPIRITS	137	S is for SHOCK
95	L is for LOSING IN EVERY WAY	138	S is for SPECIAL DAYS
98	M is for MEMORIES	140	S is for SUICIDE
99	M is for MESSAGES FROM THE OTHER SIDE	142	S is for SUN
		143	S is for SURVIVOR GUILT
101	M is for MIRROR	146	T is for TATTOOS
103	M is for MONKEY MIND	147	T is for TEARS
104	M is for MOUNTAIN OF GRIEF	150	T is for TERMINAL ILLNESS
107	N is for NIGHTMARE	153	T is for TIME
109	N is for NOTIFICATION OF NEXT OF KIN	155	T is for TRIGGERS
		158	U is for UNIQUE CELEBRATIONS OF LIFE
110	N is for NORTHERN LIGHTS		
113	O is for OFF BALANCE	160	U is for UNUSUAL PLACES TO REMEMBER YOUR LOVED ONE
114	O is for OTHER DEATHS		
116	P is for PAIN	163	V is for VAGUE
118	P is for PATTERN OF GRIEF	164	V is for VIEWING
119	P is for PERSPECTIVE and PERCEPTION	165	V is for VISITORS
		168	W is for WHAT YOU THINK INSIDE
122	Q is for QUESTIONS THAT PROBABLY WILL NEVER HAVE A SATISFACTORY ANSWER		
		170	W is for WHOLE BODY
		174	W is for WILLS
123	Q is for QUILT	177	X is the FIRST UNKNOWN
126	R is for RAGE, REVENGE, and HATE	179	Y is for YEARNING
		180	Y is for YESTERDAY
127	R is for REACTIONS and RESPONSES TO GRIEF	182	Z is for 'ZACTLY
		183	Z is for ZEN
130	R is for RELATIONSHIPS	183	Z is for ZIGZAG THOUGHTS
132	R is for RELIEF		
134	R is for RESILIENCE		

 is for ADVICE

Me: If you're fortunate, you'll get good advice, given as *suggestions and information* from good people who want to help. Please believe this: you *can* and *will* eventually take more control of your personal grief process. No one can fix or rationalize or wash away your pain with advice. All you have to do right now is breathe. Breathe deeply if you can.

- Try to stay away from coffee, as it makes you hyper, and from alcohol, as it makes you sadder, and you may say or do things that you regret later. It lowers your inhibitions.
- Try to drink milk or water or a protein drink if you can't eat.
- Try a tiny bite of dry toast or light soups. Comfort foods don't digest well right now.
- Music sometimes helps.
- Talk, holler, scream, keen, ululate, babble … whatever you feel the need to do.
- Wear soft clothes and cover yourself with a soft blanket.
- Don't be too hard on yourself—you're doing the best you can, and that's good enough.
- Get help with the paperwork.
- When you're making phone calls or having meetings with banks, the accountant, the funeral home, the utility companies, the government, and any others, have a pen and paper ready and take notes. Or have someone take notes for you. It's difficult to remember things right now. Whatever was said, you have it on paper.
- Let people help you with basic tasks, like shopping lists and whatever else you need help with.
- Use lots of lotion, as your skin will be drier. Get Kleenex with lotion in it.

- It's perfectly OK to cry. It gets rid of some of the toxins and all the other bad shit that builds up.
- Walking or other movement also helps clear your mind.
- Try to watch the sun rise and then set. It's one more day you've gotten through. Good work!
- Tell people if you do want to be hugged or not. You have the right to choose.
- Try to stay away from TV and social media as much as possible. The news, movies, and shows are usually violent or sad. If the death will be on the news, someone can tape it.
- Slowing down and taking deep breaths will help relieve tension.
- Get help with the children for your sake and theirs.
- Turn to your pets for comfort but also get help for them if needed.
- Try to hold a baby or toddler to help find joy.
- Concentrate on this minute, this hour, this day. You can do nothing about yesterday, and tomorrow will come regardless of what you think.
- Get help to find your strength to make decisions, or someone will make them for you, which may or may not be OK.
- Try to sleep, or at least rest.
- Pray or connect to the universe in your own way. Or not at all.
- See a doctor if you feel extreme continuing anxiety or are having panic attacks.
- Don't let anybody tell you how you should think or feel, or how long this should last.
- Have someone assigned to answer the door, and tell them what you want them to say.
- Have someone assigned to speak to the media if necessary. Help decide on the written statement from the family.
- Have someone assigned to look after and keep track of the food and other donations.

I suggest you DO NOT accept the following "advice" *(and the reason why)*:

- Be strong. People don't expect weakness from you. *(It's NOT weak to grieve. It's a strength.)*
- Crying in front of people makes them uncomfortable, OR There's no need to cry, OR Crying won't help. *(Uncomfortable? Too bad. Won't help? Yes, it will. It's important for you to cry.)*

- Let's go. It's time to get things done. (*Do things as best you can in your own time.*)
- You need to get out in public more. (*No, you don't. It's up to you.*)
- Your panic attacks and anxiety are all in your head. (*They are REAL things. See a doctor.*)
- You should get out of bed and visit. These people have stopped in to see you. (*If they're your friends, they'll understand. If they're not, why are they there?*)
- You need to taste the cake I made. We have to have some together right now. (*Your stomach probably can't handle sweets. Put it in the freezer for later.*)
- You'll soon be back to your old self. (*Nobody has a right to make any time frame for you, and we will never be back to who we were.*)
- Just keep busy and you won't think of it. (*They obviously have no idea.*)
- Get rid of all his (or her) clothes in the closet. They only serve as reminders. (*If you need to touch them, smell them, and remember, then do it. Take your time.*)
- It's not good to talk about it so much. It just reminds you of it. (*It's important you talk about it as much as you choose to. It helps your mind begin to slowly understand.*)
- I brought a bottle so you can drown your sorrows today. Tomorrow's a new day. (*Alcohol intensifies certain feelings, will lower your inhibitions, and you may do or say things you may regret. Plus your mind and body will both feel a lot worse when you sober up.*)
- Before you know it, you'll be fine, and this will be a distant memory. (*Again, don't let anybody set a time frame or expectations for you.*)
- You have to fight it. You can't let it hurt like this. (*Fight what? Grief will hurt regardless.*)
- Maybe it's time to move on. (*Again, it's your time and your choice. "Grief time" takes time, and each step is a BIG step, no matter how small you think it is.*)

AND SO ON ... I suggest you don't listen to this "advice," as it will unnecessarily make you feel worse.

It's not healthy to let someone try to fix you, or rationalize for you, or wash away your pain.

* * *

A is for AFTER

Me: There's always a *before*, followed by an *after*, usually marked by split second timing of a death. At first you exist in the angry and totally desolate time after.

Annabelle: It's incredibly challenging and horrible and heart-breaking to go into the *after* of death. During, and for weeks after the funeral, the decisions I had to make were overwhelming. I struggled with so much paperwork and cried when my mind came up empty. I talked to the lawyer, accountants, and bank tellers as if I were in my right mind, when I knew my right mind died with my husband. When I went home, I didn't remember what was decided, or what I was supposed to do. So I cried. I couldn't remember anything, and it scared me. So I cried. I finally accepted that I had to make some decisions. I started reading paperwork that helpful people had sent home with me. I started making lists for every phone call and meeting with lawyers, bankers, accountants, funeral direc-tors, government agencies, utilities, and all other paperwork. And then I cried. Paperwork at this time is a mean little sidebar after a death.

Alexis: His clothes were still on hangers in the closet and in the dresser drawers. What do you do with them after? Everything he owned and touched was sitting there. The house was empty and echoed of him. For the first time, my house was a painful place, but I was afraid to leave it. His aftershave that I loved hung like a sad cloud in the air after. Everything needed to be dealt with after, but how long after? Don't let anybody rush you. Some decisions will take weeks, but some will take months, even years.

Arthur: I cooked because she taught me to cook. But she didn't teach me how lonely it is to cook for one person. Food tasted like sawdust anyway, so I just didn't eat. Or I ate nothing but easy comfort food: doughnuts, bread and honey, cakes and cookies that friends and neighbors had brought over, and bags of junk food. I ate straight out of the cupboard or the fridge so that I didn't have to see the empty chair across from me. It took all my willpower to go out, as everyone averted their eyes, not knowing what to say. I dressed the same but wore a dif-ferent shell after. I had been told I radiated sorrow, no matter how nicely I tried to make my face smile. There was guilt in smiling after. And God forbid I should laugh. It sounded like a squeaky door, and I was fooling no one. But there is an after down the line that's better. You do learn it's OK to smile and laugh. And friends and Google can help you cook for one person.

Ashley: I noticed stupid little things after. His name is still in the phone book and on cell phones out there. I didn't touch the answering machine with his alive voice on it for a long time after. I felt the need to listen to it every day. I laughed and I cried because he was so silly on it.

After will not always be so chaotic:

- A long while after, you check what exists outside your purgatory. You breathe better. You make some new choices. You take some new chances. You spread your wings a bit at a time, ready to bolt but still trying.
- You slowly trust enough to let people into your heart if you haven't before. There's no set time, as this could take months. But somewhere in the future, all the little "afters" you work on will be taken in, digested, and sorted out, until you can say: "Before he died," or "After he died," with a new voice.
- You will be able to cherish and covet the before and eventually accept your different life after. This will be a different life, but you will have survived … with scars.
- There's no return to pre-death life, so you strive for a new life after the death.
- There is a transformation after that puts you in a new place in life, a transition from what you knew to what you are learning.

* * *

A is for AIR

Me: The dreaded word "dead" slams the air from you with a fierce punch.

- Everything clenches up in your chest and stomach and lungs and strangles your windpipe. Your throat suddenly holds a big ball, like somebody shoved a wool sock down there. Your bunched up airway lets air out, usually with a scream, a groan, a sigh, or a sob. And then it struggles with too little air because the air around you is too heavy to suck back in.

- Breathe. It's all you *have* to do at this traumatic moment and beyond. Drop your shoulders. Breathe in through your nose as deeply as you can. Drop your shoulders. Breathe out through your mouth. Listen to your breathing. Focus on it. In and out. In and out. Drop your shoulders. And just breathe. It becomes a focus.

Angela: I couldn't get enough air, yet somehow there was too much air inside me. I couldn't breathe. It seemed like I found myself inside a huge balloon, or maybe it was the other way around. The balloon was somewhere inside me, and it was going to explode and a million pieces of me would fly into the atmosphere. I had to hold a balloon in my hand to remind me neither thing was happening.

Al: People trying to help me were saying, "Just take a breath." I couldn't understand why they kept saying that. I didn't realize my shoulders were up around my ears, and I wasn't breathing. In and out. I discovered that everything inside is tensed up and crunched up, and just breathing becomes a second-by-second challenge. When you endlessly sigh, which you will, your body wants more air. Try taking deep breaths.

* * *

A is for ANGELS

Me: The room is full of many, many angels right now. They are unseen energy. You don't have to believe in the spirit world, because it's a very personal belief and understanding. But this is what I feel strongly. Everyone comes into this world with an angel on his or her shoulder, and every soul goes into the next world of light with an angel on his or her shoulder. So if you weren't able to be with your loved one when he or she died, it's OK to believe that he or she did not die alone. Someone beautiful, loving, and full of light was reaching out with welcoming guidance. That gives me some peace. Amen.

Me: Then there are the angels here on earth.

- They don't have wings, but they help lift your wings when you forget how to fly.
- They don't sit on a cloud, but they sit on a chair or bed in your home because you couldn't get through what you're going through without them.
- They don't play harps, but they are like a beautiful song, bringing melodies and musical notes back into your life.
- They don't share heavenly messages (or maybe they do), but their words and hugs help heal your heart and uplift your life, putting you on the new-normal path.
- They don't project heavenly beams, but they show you light at the end of the dark tunnel and walk with you towards it.
- They don't dress in heavenly raiment but wear earthly clothes.

So you might not recognize them as angels until they have stood by your side, looked in your eyes as the tears fell, quietly taken your hand, helped when you needed it, and loved you unconditionally. They are family, friends, neighbors, and maybe even strangers who have gone out of their way to show love. You are surrounded.

* * *

 is for ANIMALS

Me: I know from experience that when a pet dies, animal lovers often grieve as they would for a human friend. They loved all the things about that pet that they love about people—maybe more sometimes, as a pet loves unconditionally and seems to know when to be available and when to quietly be near. It's a loving and caring friend with eyes that "talk" to you.

Archie: A ranching friend once told me that as owners of pets, we assume the responsibility for a good life for them, indoors or outdoors, in town or on a farm. As their keepers, it's also our responsibility to help them pass from this life into the next. We don't just "get it done." We handle it with dignity, either with a vet or by ourselves on the farm. It's a gift we give back to our animals who have given us so much. And it's good to grieve them.

Angela: I was really angry when a former friend laughed because I couldn't stop crying when my dog died. I was devastated. My dog was the best friend I ever had. I knew I would miss her beautiful and dedicated personality every minute of every day. That "someone" offered to get me a new dog. That was a decent apology, but you don't just replace a pet. I want people to know that the love you feel for a pet is valid and special and should be respected. And your grief is valid and real and should also be respected.

Andy: When I was little, my dog died. I was so sad to lose my faithful companion who listened attentively to everything I said, who licked my face when I was sad, and who slept at the foot of my bed to ward off monsters. My parents helped me plan a funeral service before we buried him. They said it was OK to cry because we all feel sad when we lose our best friend. To this day, I appreciate those moments in which they taught me about grief. Last year I knew not to brush it off when my daughter had to face the death of her beloved cat.

* * *

A is for ANXIETY

Me: Anxiety, that overwhelming dark feeling, will visit you. It comes from fears about what has happened or what might happen next. It especially affects your breathing, heart rate, and thinking but can grow into a full panic attack and make you think you're dying.

Suggestions for grounding yourself to help you control anxiety:

- Breathe deeply in through your nose (new air in).
- Blow out as much as you can through your mouth (old air out).
- Look at and identify the names of five things around you.

- Reach out, touch, and identify four things near you.
- Identify three sounds around you.
- Identify two smells.
- Identify one emotion.
- Keep breathing deeply until you feel relaxed.

I hope you have successfully controlled whatever caused your anxiety at that moment. Good work!

* * *

A is for ASHES

Me: This is for those who believe in cremation and aren't sure what to do with the ashes. My husband's ashes are sitting on the buffet in a beautiful wooden box branded by a friend. When all our family is ready, half will be spread at our lake property, where he found such peace and joy, and the other half will be spread in the mountains from horseback for the same reason. Some of the ashes are in necklaces for my daughter and me. They are also in little sandy footprint urns for the grandsons. Besides the huge choice of urns, and what you can order through the funeral home, the following is a list of where others have placed (or plan to place) parts or all of their loved one's ashes:

- in a little container glued into the middle of a hand-made dream catcher
- a tattoo in which a small amount of the ashes is mixed with the ink (Check with your tattoo artist beforehand. Quite a number of people said this kept their loved one as close as possible.)
- in a columbarium or niche in the cemetery
- in an urn buried the required depth in another loved one's grave
- a painting in which a small amount of the ashes was worked into the paints (One woman, who is not an artist, also chose to do this to express her feelings on canvas.)
- a great variety of jewelry, including rings, bracelets, earrings, necklaces— anything that can hold a small sealed "pocket" of ashes

- in a sealed glass (There can be many different beautiful memorial sayings etched or inked on the glass.)
- inside a great variety of glassware shaped like birds, flowers, or whatever is symbolic for you and your loved one (This must be done by a professional glass blower.)
- under a tree so the roots will grow strong from them
- beneath a cairn of stones
- in a fire
- in a body of water
- inside a special cross, a cane, a pool cue, a sporting item, a favorite tool— whatever can be sealed and put on display in or on a cabinet or hung on the wall (Perhaps it's not a good idea to actually use any of these things, for obvious reasons.)
- a small sealed urn in a stuffed animal so you can hug it whenever you feel the need, or inside a pretty pillow that can sit close by
- in a flower bed so the beauty continues
- under a new house being built by a guy whose wife had drawn up the plans for their "forever home" before she died, and he wanted her to be as much a part of it as possible
- and so on …

Great ideas? Yes. Crazy ideas? Not to the people who talked about them. If you're putting ashes inside anything, remember that they are quite heavy, and they should be properly sealed, as they are *ashes*. Alberta released guidelines in 2019 to allow ashes to be scattered on unoccupied Crown land or water, including provincial parks. If you're not positive about the rules, talk to your funeral director. And we must all be considerate. Not everyone is as open as we are about this final disposition.

* * *

A is for ASSISTED DYING

Me: The Assisted Dying Law is seen by some people as a good law, while others believe it's a bad law. This segment of the population believes it allows for murder and gives people the right to take lives willy-nilly. Those who thinks it's a good law see it as an answer to a prayer. The arguments are such:

- Doctors and medical staff do everything possible to save a life. But a loved one doesn't have to live in excruciating pain and without a mental or physical life anymore. We put animals down that are in severe pain, but we have pills and machines that can prolong the agony for people.

- How much time on machines is too much, especially if they said earlier in life that they would *not* want to live like this? What if they held your hand and begged you to let them die?

- With Assisted Dying, you fill out a "Record of Request for Medical Assistance in Dying." There can be an approved proxy for those whose physical and/or interconnected brain dysfunctions are beyond response. The medical staff have done everything possible. They now make every effort to communicate before they allow a proxy to be involved. Two independent doctors do an assessment after the request is received, then there is a ten-day "Period of Reflection." Then you and a doctor decide the date, time, and location of death. All the information on Medical Assistance in Death can be found at ahs.ca/maid or MAID.CareTeam@ahs.ca

Ariel: We have spent our whole lives running from death. We don't want to see it, and if we must see it, we want it to be like the movies—loving, gentle, graceful, and dignified. We learned first-hand that is not reality. It is messy and painful and can be horrific. It shouldn't be with diapers and catheters and bed sores and mouth sores and cracked lips. Not with gibberish from a brain wracked by disease, and not by painful gasps with the terrible struggle to breathe. Our brain still tells us not to embrace death but to run from it, even as the reality tells us it is near. We can't make our loved one stay with us through that pain and anguish. We have to put aside our natural instincts and teachings that this is not suicide, this is not murder. This is us helping our loved ones make a decision when they have had no say since their dying process began. This was my husband saying that this was his only control over cancer. He begged for death. Was it my place to deny him that, no matter my teachings from the Sunday school of my childhood? I put aside all the teachings in my life and realized that I needed to embrace the new reality of death nearby—one without pain, without drawers full of meds, and without gasping for air. When I accepted this new reality, he became calmer, because he could see an end to his suffering. *His* suffering, not mine. *Mine* was just beginning—the pain of loss. But my pain was endurable; his was not.

Alice: My cancer-ridden sister was in a hospice for seven days before she died. In a hospice there are no heroic measures taken, but they ensure the pain is under control. After seeing her in excruciating pain for so long, it was a relief to be there—for her and for us. She was made as comfortable as possible by a gentle and caring staff, who will always be my heroes. We could stay twenty-four hours a day and sleep on a daybed beside her. It was horrible to realize she was dying but a gift that we could be with her, and that she died gently instead of writhing in pain. To us, that was assisted death as it should be.

Alphonse: You try breathing day and night through a small, semi-plugged drinking straw, begging someone to take away the pain, and you tell me that Assisted Dying is a sin. We wouldn't even let our beloved animals live like that.

Annie: I don't care if you call it Assisted Dying, or what you call it, it is wrong, and I'm totally against it. I haven't had to sit beside someone through their dying, but I would never assist them in taking their own life. That person still has a purpose. I'm sorry if it tests your love and your patience to watch them, but it's a sin against God, and it's murder no matter how you look at it, and no matter what excuses you make. You do what you can live with after.

Abraham: Very briefly, I can say that I am familiar with Assisted Dying. My mom had fought long enough and reached a point where she couldn't eat, drink, or understand anything around her. In palliative care, she was kept comfortable and pain-free. Our family was so grateful she had what we called Assisted Dying, with the utmost love, care, and dignity.

* * *

Notes

B is for BARGAINING

Me: We try to make a deal with a higher power if they will change the outcome.

Betty: I wasn't sure what I believed of God or the afterlife, but there I was on my knees, out of my mind, by my daughter's hospital bed, trying to barter with an unfamiliar power beyond me. God, if You're there, take my life, not hers. Or let her breathe again, and I'll live every moment of the Golden Rule and the Ten Commandments. *I will, I will, I will …*

Brian: You bring him back to me, and I will believe in You. I'll get out of my wheelchair and come up there and live with You and see my brother happy on earth instead of the other way around. You took the wrong brother.

Barbara: Heavenly Father, forgive my wickedness, but please listen to my prayer. I have an uncle who lives in major pain with Multiple Sclerosis and begs to die. I have a ninety-two-year-old grandmother who loved life and honored You but has had Alzheimer's for many years. I haven't had the courage to say this to anybody, but please consider a trade. You know my husband had an aneurysm. You take those two and tell me I don't have to take my life partner off life support. I need my Ben to live. Is what I'm asking for a sin?

* * *

B is for BEFORE

With most events, there's a gradual shift from before to after. But with death, there's a stark and harsh before and after. Before he died; after he died. One minute your loved one's alive and breathing. The next minute, he or she is no longer of this earth. The body is now just a shell that contains none of the living attributes of the vibrant person you knew and loved. And that's what we struggle really, really hard to understand and accept.

- What does everyone say when they talk about the recent death? They talk about the moments before. They want to discuss why this happened so fast. Or did it? They feel there must have been some indication before he or she died. They remember the last moment they saw him or her. They think they remember the last words. They remember how well he looked or how ill she looked. They want to know what led up to this, what happened just before the death.

- Then they discuss hundreds of moments with him or her. Before. That's why a funeral reception is so important. Remember what he said about …? Remember that time? He was a beautiful singer. She was an incredible volunteer. He was the best friend you could ever ask for. She was an incredible neighbor for fifty years. Nobody could wield a hammer like him. What a gem. What a card. What a loving father and grandfather. She was so proud of being a mother, grandmother, sister, aunt, cousin, and friend.

Every day around the world there are constant discussions in different countries, in different languages, about personality traits, skills, words of wisdom, and great times … before. Before death happened. After is tough. But thank God we had before. It truly helps us in our healing.

"Death ends a life, not a relationship." —Mitch Albom

* * *

B is for BELIEF

Me: A belief is a conviction you hold to be true. There are many different religious and non-religious beliefs, all to be respected. Reasons for certain beliefs are: strength, love, faith, help, fellowship, family traditions, meaning in life and death, feeling the world was created for us, social support, survival, seeking order from chaos, trusting there's a power bigger than us, or any related thoughts and feelings.

- I'm a Christian, and my son died. Maybe I didn't pray hard enough. Or maybe He didn't hear me. Or maybe I prayed for the wrong thing. I'm not sure what to believe now.
- It would be vain to believe "here" is all there is. To survive grief, I have to believe there is a good life beyond this.
- I really don't believe in anything. I'm one of those people who believed my father in the casket was all dressed up with no place to go but underground.
- If it wasn't for my strong belief in God, my faith, and my church friends, I would have gone crazy in that now-empty house. Thank you, God. Thank you, Jesus. And thank you to my minister and my church family.
- The Heavenly Father surrounds me in my grief, and even though I'm not always with Him, He is always with me. He gives me strength. I must believe that, or I'll lose my mind.
- I gave up on my religious beliefs. I was told He hadn't given up on me. So why did He let my son and my wife be killed?
- A lovely Christian woman held me to her ample bosom and told me to let Jesus take the pain and fears away. Oh, yes, please. She left. I closed my eyes and prayed: "Here's my pain, Jesus, and here are my fears. Please take them. They're too heavy for me. I can't carry them." There was no flash of light or warmth around me, and my pain and fear were still there as strong as ever. Maybe I need my friend to pray for me, because I obviously don't know the rules or methods or what you use to call on Jesus. Or maybe I'm just a dumb ass who was looking for Jesus to perform a miracle or magic.
- I let go and let God take the pain. Well, it wasn't that simple, but I prayed for strength, and I attached my heart and mind to the strength of God. There

were moments I knew He was holding my pain so I could breathe again. He didn't take my pain away: He just helped me face it.

- I didn't turn to a religious leader by any specific name. I turned to the Supreme Being in the universe, as I believe there is a healing power in everything of the earth and nature.

- I believe in God, and I don't think He makes bad things like death happen. I can't believe He reached down and turned the steering wheel when my niece was killed. My God is a loving God. I think He gives us choices, and sometimes those choices lead to death. Then He reaches down to give us strength to walk through the fires of hell here on earth.

- While I expressed my faith, I expressed my grief also. Sometimes one louder than the other.

- I'm empty of beliefs and angry at whoever's in charge up there. I feel like I was duped. I prayed for my wife to live, and she suddenly died. Maybe later on I'll have a different answer.

- For a while after, I had no beliefs. But luckily, I found someone to talk to who didn't judge me or be critical or tell me what to think. He just listened. His quietness helped me find my way back to my spiritual beliefs.

Brienna: I've always sort of believed but questioned God and the Bible. And with the death of my husband, I have even more questions. If there is this God, or whatever, why did He take a really good man off this earth? Why did He put my children through such pain and horror? Why would He say my husband is living in Heaven when we loved him so much and needed him so badly here? Why are there so many bad people perpetrating only evil on earth, yet my children don't have their good father? I have so many more questions for whoever is supposed to be up there, but right now, God and I aren't on a one-way street. I might start believing in Him again if He or someone who speaks for Him can answer my questions.

Bev: I don't think I can discuss my beliefs right now. I'm really confused about the difference between organized religion and spirituality. I believed in God, and she believed only in what she called spirituality. My only belief is that my friend is at peace in a new world.

Brown: I live like a hermit since my strong and beautiful wife died. I moved out to my cabin because I couldn't stay in the house at first. It was ours. I don't know if there's a specific God or anything everybody argues over. But I believe my spiritual strength is all around me out here in nature, where we found peace and joy. I'm so grateful that she is always near me here, thanks to my Supreme Being.

Belinda: When my twenty-eight-year-old son was losing his battle with cancer, I prayed endlessly for a miracle. He said he couldn't fight it anymore and assured me he was ready to go in peace. I would still pray silently for a miracle, and my son would lay quietly and watch me and then close his eyes, and I knew he was praying to die. Several months after his funeral, I was standing in my kitchen with tears streaming. I felt God had really let me down, and I was angry at Him. I had had such faith. The only way I can describe what happened next is I suddenly felt a warm presence, a soft aura wrapping its arms around me. A voice said quietly, "I couldn't answer both your prayers, so I answered his. I am still with you." It was a powerful message. It gave me peace and a strong belief that now God and my son are both with me always.

Me: That is the beauty of freedom of choice. I believe there is an energy beyond us that we can tap into when our energy and strength are failing and we're afraid our faith in the universe has died with our loved one. Some people have tremendous, unfailing faith at this time, and I envy them. Others turn away from their faith, believing it has just let them down. Whatever you call this Spiritual Being, He or She or It, it is yours to communicate with as you need to at the moment. Hang on to whatever is yours and know that the energy of the universe will always be there for you.

* * *

B is for BLACK ARMBANDS

Me: Just a thought. People in mourning no longer wear black armbands, and that's a shame. When they were used, it signified you weren't your usual self because a loved one had died. You were sad, angry, or lost because you were grieving. Your black armband gave you rights. People paid proper attention to it.

They understood if you didn't want to stop and talk, if you didn't want to smile and chat, if you didn't want to go to an event. They didn't tell you it was time to move on. They didn't tell you that you shouldn't feel a certain way. Sports teams use them now as a show of honor for a player or coach who died. They still garner respect and revive memories, and that's a wonderful group action. But individuals don't wear them anymore. Why not?

Brielle: Yes! I not only wanted to wear a black armband—I wanted to go the full route: dressing completely in black, with a long dress and a veil to cover my face, and a crocheted shawl for comfort. I didn't want people to see my face, especially my eyes, because I felt they were blank and puffy and red, and they wouldn't stop leaking tears. When you're covered all in black, no one should approach you; you shouldn't have to speak except to the people you choose; all your paperwork should be done for you; and so on. And I'd like that to last about a year. Then I could manage in the world and wear bright colors. Seriously.

Me: Queen Victoria ordered her royal servants to wear black crepe armbands for at least *eight years* after the death of her beloved husband, Albert. Wikipedia notes President Franklin D. Roosevelt wore a black armband mourning the recent death of his mother at the time he signed the declaration of war against Japan in December 1941. The first baseball team to wear black armbands was the Boston Americans, on March 31, 1907 with the death of their manager (baseballhalloffame.org).

* * *

B is for BLAME

Me: We always need answers, and we need to place blame when there's a death. We put that responsibility on anybody and everybody.

- What do you mean, it "just happened?" How come they were all traveling together?
- How come her cancer was never detected before?

- How come you let her go out with that asshole? Was he that suspicious little jerk we saw earlier hangin' around there, and what did he do?
- How come you let her marry that son of a bitch?
- How come you fed him so much junk food with fats and creams and all that shit in it?
- How come you let him smoke and bought him cigarettes?
- How come you did drugs with him?
- How come you did it? How come you did it? How come you did it? You shoulda, you coulda, if you woulda.

The above are all dangerous questions to ask another person in your relationship who is also grieving. They suggest blame.

Then we expand the blame:

- If she had gotten in to see the doctor earlier, she wouldn't have died.
- It's that goddamn government.
- If he hadn't been teased, he wouldn't have completed suicide. It's those goddamn kids at school and the teachers who don't stop it.
- If she would have gone in for the blood transfusion, she'd be fine. It's that goddamn religion of hers.
- If he didn't eat so much fat and sweets and junk food, he wouldn't have died of a heart attack.
- It's the goddamn suppliers … and media … and advertising.
- If the police would have taken her complaints seriously sooner, she'd still be alive.
- If he hadn'ta met that guy in high school, he wouldn'ta been into drugs. It's the goddamn drug dealers. Nobody looks after anybody anymore.
- If he hadn't smoked two packs a day, he wouldn't have died of lung cancer. It's those goddamn money-grubbing tobacco companies.
- If that doctor had diagnosed and treated this earlier, she would still be alive.

It's not up to outsiders to judge whether those "reasons" are actually true, but grievers feel somebody has to take the blame, or else none of this makes sense. SOMEBODY is responsible, right or wrong.

A lot of the above seems perfectly legitimate at the time. We're mad. We're scared. We're in pain. Somebody has to pay. But experience says doctors, teachers, police, and other professionals are not causing deaths. They're sadly dealing with the fallout.

* * *

B is for BREAKING BREAD

Me: Bread has been called comfort food, the staff of life, the Body of Christ, and a delicious trigger of sweet moments. In our household growing up, it was a joy for us six kids to wolf down bread like it was candy. We were holding a little bit of Heaven with that fresh, hot bread slathered with butter and honey, or Roger's Golden Syrup. It felt so deeply cozy and safe to be in that house with that family on bread-baking and bread-breaking days.

The healing power of bread and the phrase to "break bread" took on a whole new meaning the night of the shooting deaths of our four RCMP officers on March 3, 2005. The survivors from the small RCMP detachment where I worked looked out on a suddenly strange and extremely painful world together. At the same time, everyone was trying to look inward to find any sense of balance or reasoning in a world gone mad.

And now I was walking into my own home, alone, at 3:00 a.m. The quiet of the house, usually welcoming, now reminded me I was bringing the noisy horror of the murders into our home. Everything that had been so familiar in my world that morning was now foreign. I couldn't shed what I was carrying, and everything about me felt heavy. Overloaded.

Then my eyes rested on the braided bread. I picked it up. It wasn't foreign. It was the humble center of a hearty meal. It was the center of a happy home. At that moment, it was the center of my universe. It was all I could focus on and all I could see.

I cradled it to me and heard a deep, throaty sound. It was me. There were tears falling on it. Thank you for this dose of goodness in this suddenly crazy world. It was the bread that my friend Annie makes, light and heavenly. In my mind, it still carried the fresh-from-the-oven warmth and lingering fragrance.

I tore a piece off. I knew this goodness from my childhood. I was back in my mom's warm kitchen with the beautiful smells and tastes of her bread. Oh, how I wanted to be back there, in the safe kitchen of my childhood before the shooting.

I lifted the piece of bread to my mouth, but suddenly I knew there wasn't room in my throat for the lump of pain and the bread. So I broke a smaller piece off and stood with two precious gifts in my hands. I felt the immense value of breaking bread with a friend, whether she was in front of me or at home in bed in the middle of the night thinking of all of us.

My husband came into the kitchen and held me. "I can't swallow it," I cried into his solid shoulder.

"It's OK," he said for the first of a thousand times. "It's OK. Annie left it with love. You don't have to swallow it. It's OK."

It was the breaking of bread that told me that love and support come in many forms and in many little pieces after a tragedy. Just take one small piece at a time and do what you can.

* * *

B is for BUCKET LIST

Breanna: I asked my terminally ill husband if he wanted to make a bucket list. "I don't want a bucket list," he said. "I just want to spend as much time with you, our kids, and grandkids as I'm able. Fishing, going out for a meal, talking about what excites them, listening to their future plans, sharing memories, and just watching them and all of you live."

Barkley: After my wife died, I opened the surprise bucket list she had written for me. At the top was something difficult to do for the first little while, but I'm working on it. It said, "Don't live small and quiet just because I've died. Live big and noisy like we always did, because *you* are still alive." The second one will be easier: "Listen for me talking to you. And feel me close by, as I'm gone, but I will never leave you." And the third was, "Keep watching all of our loved ones grow and live well, and remember, *we started this together.*" There were other things on the list. It included house stuff, trips, activities, and silly stuff she thought I would enjoy. I haven't done them, because the first three are my everyday focus. And that list from her reminded me why I loved every day of our fifty-one years together.

Bean: When my husband became bed-ridden but still had all his mental faculties, we daily went on trips around the world with Google. At night, I would have him make a bucket list of where he wanted to "travel" the next day. Together, every place he picked became the most interesting place in the world. We even virtually "shopped" in the most expensive places and "ate" in the best restaurants. Just before he died, he handed me a bucket list of places I had never heard of and asked me to promise to continue our "trips." The best promise he left at the bottom of the list was that he would be there beside me. And on my final trip, he would be my guide when we were reunited.

* * *

Notes

C is for CANDLES

Me: I discovered there are many reasons to light candles when our minds are in turmoil. Each spring in The Fallen Four Memorial Park in Mayerthorpe, Alberta, there is a candlelight vigil, momentarily driving away the darkness in our community.

We look to the light of candles to remember our men: Cst. Peter Schiemann, Cst. Leo Johnston, Cst. Brock Myrol, and Cst. Anthony Gordon, the four RCMP officers shot and killed on March 3, 2005. The candles are lit from five large candles burning inside the building—four for our men, and one for ALL other uniformed officers across Canada who no longer carry the flame of life but live in our hearts as heroes we carry the flame for.

It is a sanctuary of love, with people holding candles and surrounding the center obelisk and four bronze statues in the park. It's an opportunity for hearts to bring to mind those who join the circle in spirit only.

Candles represent the light of quiet faith, the light of courage, the light of remembrance, the light of hope for the future, and the strongest of all, the light of love. Candles are for solitude, contemplation, and reflection. They help us meditate in our minds and hearts, and help us focus, to still our busy minds.

To the five bronze monuments that rise in our Fallen Four Memorial Park in honor of lives well lived by our heroes and lost way too soon, we lift our candles, our prayers, our hearts, and our thoughts to all.

May you light candles anywhere, anytime, and focus on what candles can bring to your mind and heart as you grieve. The world at that moment is no bigger than the candle flame. That's all there is right now.

When you choose to blow out your candles, transfer the flame of love, memory, courage, and hope to your heart, mind, and soul to carry with you throughout the year.

> *"Candles for tempest-tossed days, candles of grace to ease heavy burdens, candles of love to inspire all my living; candles of joy despite all sadness; candles of hope where despair keeps watch; candles of courage when fear is present. Candles that will burn all the year long." —Howard THURMAN*

* * *

C is for CAREGIVERS

Me: There are many categories of splendid caregivers in the world. This is for the people who become caregivers at home for the weeks or months leading up to the inevitable death of a loved one.

- The dying person moves from a healthy, vibrant member of the household to a very dependent and often angry individual. It's a bitch for both in the equation. "We" becomes "me" and "you" when the terminally ill become invalids. Often the old relationships are quietly shredded in the process.
- There is a total focus by the caregiver on the patient: medications around the clock, meals in whatever form, bowel movements on time, and physical and mental exercises as recommended. Diapers challenge dignity. Even having visitors is difficult. The focus is entirely on living and dying.
- The hours in a day belong to the agenda of the dying. The whole house and the atmosphere in it belong to the dying.

A friend whose husband is dying of cancer said she feels home is the only logical choice for her husband, as love and marriage are forever, in sickness and in health. A lot of people don't understand why caregivers feel such a deep need to do what they do. Caregivers DO understand.

For my friend, it's twenty-four-hour care for this previously kind and gentle man who is a shadow of the robust and happy man she married. When does she sleep? When does she eat? When does she get to replenish all she has lost or given away? When does she have a different conversation other than meds and dying? When should she call the ambulance? She's exhausted mentally and physically. But she said Home Care and her health care team make it easier.

To all of you caregivers, I have such respect for you. It's a bitch of a job, full of more intense highs and lows than you'll ever feel again. Your shoulders are carrying a weight no one should have to experience. But I know most of you just want to "keep on keepin' on," even when your loved one is moved to a medical facility. A hospice nurse said that when the dying move into the hospice, they move beyond the pain. It belongs only to the caregiver now. Caregivers, please allow *yourselves* to heal.

Connie: I was exhausted and anxious all the time and had no idea how long this would last. I wanted it to be me suffering through this journey of death rather than him. I admit that sometimes I had a niggling thought that it was time it was all over. Of course, the feeling of guilt that followed made me feel like a bitch. An expert in this field helped me with my guilt by convincing me that what I was feeling was "normal."

Carl: I have to admit that I was relieved when my wife asked to be moved to the hospital. When she was at home, I was lost. I felt like I failed her miserably some days. I didn't know how to do this. There were people helping, and the Home Care nurse was good, but I was scared each time she left. It was better for both of us when my wife was moved to a hospital and had the real caregivers looking after her. Then I knew she was getting topnotch care. I will always be indebted to them.

> "A Prayer for Caregivers: When life feels too hard and the way seems unclear, please give them strength to keep on keeping on. Amen." —Women Working

* * *

C is for CHILDREN and DEATH

Me: As a society, we don't talk about death much in our homes. We removed the human touch from death years ago. Back then it was a family affair, with children allowed into the discussion. The body was prepared at home and viewed. Death was part of life. Now funeral homes must do the preparation. Blessedly, some of them encourage children to be part of the funeral plans. Children grieve in their own way, each one differently, no matter their age. They also deal with their grief through play. My grandsons, ages three, five and seven, were open to discussion of their view of death, where they think Papa went, and how they remember him. At the great funeral home we used, the grandchildren all drew pictures on his "box" before he was cremated. The two older ones wrote wonderful messages for Papa to take with him. Three months later, they made and decorated a cake for his birthday. The three-year-old said, "But Papa's dead, Nanny. Didn't you remember?" I assured him I remembered, and the seven-year-old said, "It's still his birthday even if he's dead, and he can see us blow out the candles for him." Our grandchildren are so innocent. They bring good challenges with their questions, and they bring such joy with their memories.

For all the following, take into consideration the age of the child and the relationship to the deceased.

- What do you tell them? You tell them the facts briefly, without going into great detail. This depends on their age. There is a mystery about death that you can help relieve or solve.
- Ask them what they're thinking, but don't demand an answer.
- Use the words "dead" and "died" rather than euphemisms so the child fully understands.
- Use the deceased's name or nickname freely.
- Tell them briefly what happens now with the funeral. Again, help them with the mystery of death.
- Ask them to share their fears. And share yours so they know it's OK.
- Explain about crying when you're sad, and that even adults cry, but it's OK.

- Continue with routine as much as possible. If a child wants to go to school, let him or her go. But if there's a change of heart, bring him or her home.
- Reinforce that you and many others love them deeply and will take good care of them.
- Encourage them to talk about their feelings and talk briefly about your own. This is so they will know it's OK to feel whatever they feel. Feelings are neither right nor wrong. They just are.
- Allow them to comfort you if they choose to; to show caring is a two-way street.
- Children should be encouraged to add to the funeral plans. They may want their own ways to say goodbye, such as artwork, or a letter, or a favorite toy.
- Understand that children often grieve and sort out their feelings through play.
- Your library, your health unit, and your funeral home often have books you can read to a child on loss and grief. Google is also a source of information.
- Should children be taken to a funeral? What is the relationship to the deceased? Is there a supportive adult with them who will take them out if needed? Have you properly prepared them by explaining what they may hear or the tears they may see or how the room may be set up? Are they mature enough to understand when you explain the reason for a funeral and what will happen? Do they want to go? Is there an open coffin? If so, prepare them for that also. Always deal with them honestly. Take a book or other distraction if the service gets too long for them.
- Do not *force* any child to go to the funeral, to see the dead person in the coffin, or especially kiss the dead person. I know that has been done.

To help your child further, please do NOT say the following:

- Grandpa went to sleep. (*They don't want to die, so they will be afraid to go to sleep.*)
- The doctor couldn't fix him. (*Please explain why, or the child will be afraid to go to a doctor.*)
- He went to hospital and he died. (*Please explain the difference between dying in a hospital and going to get something fixed in a hospital, or the child will fight you like a banshee if you try to take him or her there for any reason.*)
- God needed a good man in Heaven (*They're afraid to be good, as that's who God takes.*)

- God just decided it was his time and took him. (*What clock did He use? Now they're scared of having no control over time, and they may hide the clocks in the house.*)
- They put her in a magic box and took her to Heaven. (*Magic? Then can she come back in the same magic box?*)
- They went away for a long time. (*Where? Why didn't they say goodbye? How long is long? Does that mean they'll come back?*)
- An angel came down from Heaven in the night and took her to be with God. (*They're not going to sleep, worrying that an angel might get them.*)

In Alan Wolfelt's little card "My Grief Rights—For Kids" he says:

- I have the right to:

  - have my own unique feelings about death

  - talk about my grief whenever I feel like talking

  - show my feelings of grief in my own way

  - need other people to help me with my grief, especially grown-ups who care about me

  - get upset about normal, everyday problems

  - have "griefbursts"

  - use my beliefs about my god to help me deal with my feelings of grief

  - figure out why the person I loved died

  - think and talk about my memories of the person who died

  - move forward and feel my grief and, over time, to heal

Children are observant little beings. They follow our lead. They need to know crying and feeling sad are OK, and they need to know they are safe and loved and there's still a life in their home and in their society. It's our responsibility as adults to ensure they get the honesty, love, information, and security they need.

Talk to your funeral director or mental health provider regarding dealing with the grief of a child.

* * *

C is for CLOSURE AFTER COURT

Me: I hear it all the time: people need "closure" with this court case. I feel that's the wrong word because it means shutting something or sealing something. A door, not a mind. There's a step completed, a court case over. But "court adjourned" is just the next step in grieving and trying to accept the fallout of the verdict. If the person you need to see go to jail is found not guilty, there is a rage to deal with. If the person is found guilty, it doesn't matter what the sentence is—it's never enough, because it won't bring your loved one back.

Cecile: I stupidly listened to the media, who said I was looking forward to closure after the court case verdict. My family and I believed that once the court case was over, there would be closure. But there wasn't. Nothing ended, because there was so much involved in the death. We just then began to process it all and what the verdict meant to our family. My daughter was still dead, and the guilty asshole was still alive. And we just then started to figure out details and grieve all over again.

Chris: We were divorced five years ago, but my ex-wife and I were still kind of friends. I was giving her a ride to her cousin's when a drunk driver hit us, and she was killed. I should have felt closure after the court found him guilty. But instead, I questioned my fault in the divorce and my memories of the crash. Court just opened up a whole new world of things for me to deal with. I finally had to go for counseling, but I wouldn't call my situation "closure." I would call it trying to make my life better with acceptance of what happened.

Carrie: I thought when they found the body, and eventually the murderer, and it went to court, I would have closure. There's never closure. There was a tragic relief I could lay my husband's body to rest properly. There was relief the person responsible would be in jail for a long time. There was a difficult acceptance of the details I had to hear. My grief came back, but it was much shorter this time. But there's no "closure," and it's been eight years. It's never really *closed* in my life.

* * *

C is for COMPARATIVE GRIEF

Me: *PLEASE, DO NOT EVER COMPARE GRIEF.* This is a sad reality. I have heard people from "the outer circle" tell a family member how their own grief was a little worse than others for whatever reason. I define the outer circle as people secondary to those closest to the deceased.

- At my daughter's funeral, a supposed friend of hers, but a stranger to me, hugged me, weeping about how devastated she was. Supposedly she lost her best friend and needed me to comfort and console her. I thought about it after and realized she wasn't a friend of my daughter but an acquaintance who seemed to be using my daughter's death to make a public display of being included in our grief.
- I may be a bitch for describing it this way, but there was one self-centered person among the "caring" at the funeral reception who was wandering from person to person, comparing her grief to ours. Hearing this acquaintance talk like this triggered an anger in me. I asked my friend to quietly suggest she stop that or else leave. How dare she compare?
- I was a nurse at a hospital when extended family arrived because a little boy was killed. One auntie had been drinking, and one was just a mouthpiece. They did everything they could to loudly outdo each other on how grief had hit them, who had been hurt the most extravagantly, and so on. Like, "Oh, yeah, well I ..." It was terrible. As I was walking over to ask them to take it outside, a husband took his wife by the arm and pulled her to their vehicle. I could list all the comparisons they made—screaming the loudest, falling down, and so on—but suffice to say, their actions appalled me.

- There is always one person in every death situation who wants everybody to know he or she had suffered death before, and his or her grief was worse than anybody else's. Whether it's the time, the place, the relationship, the number of people, the manner of death, the person brings it up and compares it to today's death. You can do one of three things: nod and listen and then walk away, tell him or her to please shut up, or ask him or her to leave. It's your right.

Every person's loss of life is horrible and has terrible circumstances around it. But at this moment, it is not about you in the "outer circle." Not their grief. Not their loss. Not who hurts the most. Not who's the loudest or most demanding. Just the grief that is ripping the actual loved ones apart. It's the only thing that matters at this moment. Please let it be their personal time, even if you have to find a way to remove someone from the room. It can and should be done.

C is for COURAGE

Me: The high school auditorium looked all shimmery through the tears, and you could almost forget for a second why you were here. It was to celebrate the graduation of an energetic young woman who wouldn't be here. A car crash three weeks before had seen to it she was no longer of this earth.

Her beautiful emerald-green grad dress was hanging limply on a hanger in her empty room, and her grad photos were being clutched by aunties and uncles who came to support her mom and dad. By their presence, Mom and Dad wanted this grad class to know it was OK to celebrate their big day. Death had taken their friend, but life was about to envelop each one of them in the arms of the future.

Everyone watched these radiant and handsome young men and women coming down the steps and onto the stage to accept their scrolls. Cameras flashed and parents cried with pride. Friends cheered and the audience applauded.

Her name was read from the list. There was a pause. Piercing silence. Even though you knew better, you automatically waited a moment for this beautiful, freckled athlete with the long red hair to step down. But you knew the shiny green dress still hung limply on a hanger, never to be worn by her.

A big man stood up from the crowd and marched, shoulders high, head high, to the stage. Dad. A big man in more ways than one. He was handed her scroll. Again, there was total silence while he shook hands with the principal. Then he slowly raised his work-worn farmer's hand in a salute to the newly-adult children beneath the caps and gowns.

One clap echoed through the auditorium. Then another. And another. The wave of sound grew. One person rose. And another. And another. They all stood in tribute to the empty seat on the bleachers and the dad with head held high, making his way back to his chair. His shoulders shook and tears made two dark paths on the chest of his light grey suit jacket. He and his grief sat down gently and grasped the waiting hand of his wife.

Dad and Mom slipped out the door shortly after, avoiding becoming the center of attention, wanting the grads and their families to take it from here.

In that one moment with the one empty stair and the one empty chair, everyone learned what "forever" means. And with that one trip to the stage and back for Dad, everyone learned the true depth of love and courage.

> *"If the people we love are stolen from us, the way to have them live on is to never stop loving them."* —James O'Barr

> *"Grief: Just because you carry it well doesn't mean it's not heavy."* —unknown

> *"If your path demands you to walk through hell, walk as if you own the place."* —unknown, Facebook

* * *

Notes

_____

_____

_____

_____

_____

_____

_____

_____

_____

_____

_____

_____

_____

_____

_____

_____

D is for DEFINITIONS

Me. I've chosen a few words that you may be curious about that can help you or those around you. The definitions come from an old *Webster's Desk Dictionary of the English Language* – 1983

> **Bereave**: *"to deprive ruthlessly or by force; to deprive by death."* Bereavement is the experience of having been deprived of that person.

> **Compassion:** *"a deep feeling of sympathy for another's suffering."* This mixes boundaries of respect. Here's what's OK for me and what's not.

> **Empathy:** *"identification with or vicarious experiencing of the feelings or thoughts of another person."* This needs boundaries. You are feeling with them and thinking with them and touching a place that says: "You're not alone. I'm here."

> **Grief:** *"keen mental suffering over loss."* The mental and physical response to being deprived of a loved one. The synonyms for grief are: sorrow, misery, sadness, anguish, pain, distress, torment, affliction, suffering, heartache, broken-hearted, heaviness of heart, woe, desolation, despondency, dejection, angst, mortification, lament remorse, regret, pining, blues, dolor.. Every single one of them is heavy and hard on the heart.

> **Mourning:** *"the conventional manifestation of sorrow for a person's death; the outward tokens of such sorrow, as black garments; a period of time during which a death is mourned."* The psychological processes you use to come to terms with your loss and getting used to a world without your loved one in it.

Pain: *"bodily suffering or distress; a distressing sensation in a particular part of the body; mental or emotional suffering or torment."* A few of many words related to pain are: sharp, piercing, throbbing, shooting, gnawing, anguish, ripping, deep, agonizing, torturous, gut-wrenching, and so on.

Sympathy: *"the ability to share the feelings of another, especially in sorrow or trouble; a relationship between persons or things whereby whatever affects one also affects the other."* I will take on your pain; whatever affects you will affect me.

* * *

D is for DENIAL

Me: When I found my husband dead after being hit by a tree, at first I went into shock. I didn't deny that he was dead, but I denied I had found him and insisted he had been in a car crash. When the shock finally wore off, my mind wanted to deny he was dead. I heard him in the kitchen or coming in the door, or laughing in another room. I had to keep reminding myself that it couldn't be. I often thought, *He's dead? Well, that's not possible.* I reached a point where I couldn't deny it, but still, after two years, I am often surprised to think about him dead.

This is a partial list of different versions of what people told me about their own denial:

- No, he's not dead. He's in his bed asleep.
- I had to deny she was dead for quite a while, until my brain couldn't deny it anymore. I counted on my denial to preserve my sanity.
- No, you can't be talking about my sister. She would never drink and drive.
- Can't be him; we have plans to go on a cruise in two weeks.
- Not him; he doesn't own a gun.
- All I did was deny, deny, deny and argue that it wasn't her.

- No! Get out of here with your lies.
- No, no, somebody that big and strong doesn't die. Does. Not. Get. Killed. Period!
- (When I went to identify her) No, no, no, that doesn't look like her at all. (It was her.)
- Not her. She hasn't been depressed. She would never take too many pills.
- It can't be her. She's meeting me for dinner later.
- I denied and denied and denied because I couldn't accept that it was real. I couldn't.
- I sat in mute disbelief for a whole day, the word "no" the only thing in my head.

* * *

D is for DIFFERENCES

Me: Differences? EVERYWHERE! EVERYTHING! Everything inside and outside our house, the cabin he built, and the playground he built for the grandchildren. Everything in the garage: all his building tools, the paint, the lathe, the gardening supplies, construction supplies, work clothes and boots, his work trailer and the hundreds of things in it, everything that his strong hands had touched and left fingerprints on. Me? I'm very different.

- Sleeping, waking, socializing, talking, decision-making, money management, traveling near and far, visiting with children, playing with grandchildren, arguing, forgiving, holding hands and kissing, supporting non-profits, cooking, eating, sharing eye contact, sharing sadness and laughter, sharing stories, making love, that warm touch, watching TV shows and movies, fixing what's broken, reading books. It really doesn't end.
- Each room in the house screams major differences: his big chair, the couches, the table arrangement, the big bed, the closets, the workout room, the laundry room, the "comfort room" on the deck, the storage room, and many more shared spaces. Every single thing in *my* life, which used to be *our* life, is different in ways you can't imagine until you're living it. Every single thing

around me and in me is painfully different and blatantly changed. This is the "new normal" I have to work on getting used to. But it really is good advice to not get rid of anything or make any big decisions for at least a year. I think it will be more than that. I don't even know where to start.

- You have lost a total lifestyle and the total present and planned future together. You haven't only lost many of the things I mentioned already, but you've lost your identified role as mom, dad, sister, brother, lover, husband, wife, daughter, son, grandma, grandpa, friend, neighbor, in-law, confidante, girlfriend, boyfriend, auntie, uncle, cousin, teacher, caregiver, provider, and happy couple. You have to re-learn what all that means now, and for the rest of your lifetime work on making the necessary changes, due to the differences. I have to tell myself many times every day: "Keep working on it. You *can* do it."

- I realized one day that I had been pushed through the door where a big black neon sign flashed "WIDOW." I hate that label. But legally, that's my new role.

Darold: I thought if I did everything I could think of, and made quick changes, the differences wouldn't be as noticeable. That was wrong. I still came home to no sound, no greeting, and no life. I finally got help to talk about how different my life actually was and is.

Me: I realize constantly: I have lost the ability to make any more memories with him. He will always be in a time and place in my memory and my heart. There are no new shares. His name is in the phone book and on cells, but he will never answer or change his message.

> *"Everything is different, you are different, the air is different, everybody around you is different, your home is different. Your world is gone. Its dimensions shrink to a smaller dimension." —unknown*

Me: YOU CAN DO IT: It may be weeks, months, or years from now, but there are differences and losses that are considered good to be rid of, that you will eventually lose after all your initial hard losses:

- your many fears of so many things you struggle with and feel beaten down with (*The difference will be your feeling of courage as you rise above your fears.*)

39

- your feeling of inability to cope (*The difference will be pride that you CAN cope, using your recently-learned coping skills.*)
- your initial feeling of ignorance of paperwork (*The difference is when you realize you CAN do paperwork; you have learned from people around you, plus your accountant or lawyer.*)
- your inability to plan the future (*There will be a different you and a different future that you have learned to plan in big and small ways.*)
- your feeling of inability to do things alone without the previous shared role (*Your new roles are different, but you have returned to some previous ones. The difference was gradual.*)
- the complete stoppage at death of the lifestyle you were used to (*Your lifestyle is new and different, but it's a process you are handling. You are making the best life now in what was the worst.*)
- your physical illnesses, whether real or psychosomatic (*Now you feel different—stronger and almost pain-free. A big difference is that you can eat better, sleep better, and breathe better.*)
- your feeling of responsibility for the feelings of others, or of hiding your grief from, and for, others (*You can think of this very differently: "I actually don't care what people think of me as I grieve now. I do it my way, and sometimes that doesn't appear pretty or normal."*)
- your deep feelings of internal pain (*These took their toll, but the difference is that they have now lessened. New and more positive feelings have entered your life.*)
- your feeling of living forever with your initial reactions and responses (*All of them were normal at the time, but there are new responses and behaviors. In this journey, you will move from being in pieces to being somewhat at peace.*)

* * *

D is for DO TELL ME ...
D is for DON'T TELL ME ...

Many people find talking to grieving people very difficult, especially at the funeral reception or shortly afterwards when you see them on the street or in the grocery store. It feels so uncomfortable for all involved. And that's OK, because everything has changed.

The conversation with them out in public used be an exchange of information about each other's family. Now it hardly seems appropriate under the circumstances.

Nobody can tell you exactly what to say, but sometimes people say things without thinking the grieving person will take offense. It's not mean or bad or stupid. Not at all. They want to help, and hope that what they're saying will soothe the soul. But there are reasons these are not always appropriate:

- God needed him. (*Not nearly as bad as I needed him.*)
- It's God's will. We learn from it. (*No. My God was a loving God. This is too cruel of a lesson.*)
- How are you? (*How do you think I am? I can't even begin to describe it to you.*)
- She's safe in the arms of Jesus. (*She was safe in MY arms, and that's where she should have stayed.*)
- Jesus takes only the best. (*He could bloody well have taken some of the murderers and rapists and violent people. Wouldn't it make more sense to take the worst from earth and leave the best?*)
- I bet she's happy in Heaven. (*She was HAPPY here.*)
- God needed another angel. (*If God's the creator, why couldn't He just create another angel and leave mine here by my side?*)
- Let's pray. (*Bugger off. I'm a lot mad at God right now.*)
- Be thankful you got those few minutes to say goodbye. I didn't get that. (*You think that makes this less painful? And don't compare your grief to mine. I have nothing left over for you right now.*)
- You need to meet my wife's friend who lost her husband. She's a good looker. (*You offensive, insensitive bastard. Do you not realize I want my wife back, not some replacement?*)
- It must have been his time. (*You don't know any such thing, or any such plan.*)
- You'll be OK. There are lots of single seniors' activities to take part in, even a singles' cruise. (*How dare you? Don't you think it's a little bit SOON?*)
- I understand. I know exactly how you feel. (*You don't have a f* * *ing clue what is going through my head and my soul right now. This is MY pain, MY thought pattern, and MY grief. You can't see inside me.*)

41

- You need to get back out into life. (*You need to leave me alone and let ME make decisions.*)
- At least you have two more children to focus on. (*SHE was our child too. SHE was our precious child whom we loved more than life itself. We love our other children more than life itself also, but she is not just an extension of our other children. She was an individual. SHE was SHE.*)
- *After a miscarriage:* There must have been something wrong for you to expel it. You're lucky you lost the fetus now instead of after it was born and you started to love it. (*It? That was my baby. Lucky? I loved that little bud growing inside me from the first moment I knew of her existence. I have every right to grieve.*)
- *After a stillbirth:* Thank Heaven this didn't go on for days, as it would be harder to let go. (*Get the fuck out of my room.*)
- You're young. You can have more. (*I don't want a replacement! I want my child.*)

Suggestions that people have given me of words that do help at the funeral reception or in the grocery store or the post office—wherever there's a short chance encounter:

- *It's good to see you. I think of you often.*
- *How are practical things at your house? Need anything done there?*
- *Just want you to know my heart is with you.*
- *Anything I can help you with? Shopping? Cooking? Child care? Housecleaning?*
- *There isn't much I can say. Is it all right if I give you a hug instead?*
- *If you want a quiet place to escape to, my house is available 24/7.*
- *Just want you to know, I always think of* (deceased's name) *with a smile.* (It's important you say the deceased's name. That's who she or he was. That is still his or her identity.)
- *Just want you to know* (deceased's name) *will be missed.*

There are many other things to say, depending on how well you knew the deceased or the griever. But there are other things I've quoted from people who are grieving.

- "Don't cross the street when you see me. When you avoid me, I feel like I've done something wrong. Just pass me by and nod or smile."

- "Don't use that whispery, smarmy voice when you talk to me. It sounds too much like pity. I hate pity."
- "Look me in the eye. I need to know I'm not a crazy person to be afraid of."
- "Say my daughter's (son's, husband's, wife's, father's, mother's) name. I love hearing it."
- "Don't give me advice unless I ask for it."
- "Don't be afraid of me and get all nervous when I'm around."
- "Don't ask questions about the death unless I initiate the conversation. Maybe I don't want to share details yet. Or ever."
- "Don't tell me how I should or shouldn't feel. Just let me feel."
- "Don't forget him." Don't forget. Please, please don't forget."

> *"In the presence of death we stand awkward and ill at ease, for death is a well-known stranger whom we recognize but do not wish to know."* —Rodney Murphy

* * *

D is for DUTY

Diane: My husband's father was not a lovable man, but all the siblings had visited because of their mother. Now they were helping plan the funeral, as they felt it was their duty to their mom. They swallowed the past and did a great job of it. They all felt sad because they didn't feel sad. My husband told his siblings after the burial that he had looked around the grave and thought, *We all did our duty to Mom, but with that shovelful of dirt on his casket, we all just buried a shitload of problems. How sad is that?*

Darryl: Before Dad died, he made me promise I would help him with two things. One was to ensure Mom was looked after, as her Alzheimer's had advanced well beyond where he could look after her. And two was to make sure that he was cremated. I knew Mom had assumed she and her "Darling" would be buried next to each other in the local cemetery. And Dad had always said, "Deedee, my love, we'll always be together, no matter where our old shells are disposed of." Dad saw cremation as the only way to defeat the cancer that was killing him. Burn it. And it was my duty to see that it was done. Three weeks later, he died. I had Dad cremated. I kept his urn. When Mom died, we knew she didn't want cremation. We put Dad's urn next to her in her coffin before it was lowered into the ground. I did my duty. They are buried side by side.

* * *

Notes

E is for EASY DEATH

Me: I was given the gift of holding my friend's hand when she died after a fairly long illness. It was a quiet and gentle death. The only way I can describe it is that her hand suddenly felt heavier in mine. And there was no movement of her lips to show she was breathing.

I had worked with this friend at the newspaper office for fifteen years, and we had the usual laughter and tears and fights and sharing of lives. We used to often be late leaving work, and her husband would come pick her up for supper. I can't count the number of times I heard her say, "OK, I think I'm ready." And his reply would *always* be, "It's about time. What took you so long?"

He died several years before her, and although she stayed busy in her life until her eighties, she missed her best friend and life partner a lot. While I waited for the nurse to determine her heart had stopped, a quick and clear picture came into my mind. I saw a strong hand reach down from a big billowy white cloud, and as my friend reached up to clasp it, a voice said, "It's about time. What took you so long?"

* * *

E is for EMPTY

Me: There are so many things that are empty when you lose a loved one. Every room in your house and everything in it feels empty. But the worst thing to deal with is the emptiness in your mind, your heart, and every fiber of your being. It's like a black hole was dug inside you, and nothing or nobody can fill it, so you just carry it around.

Me: After my husband died, our grandson, who was four at the time, looked around Papa's house as he sat sadly on the couch across from me. Staring out the window, he said quietly, "It's so different without Papa. I feel so empty." God, it broke my heart. I just nodded to agree with his adult-like perception and his wisdom. His dad came over and sat beside him, put his arm around him, and said, "I feel the same, buddy. You're right." It was so painful to see them so sad and not be able to change it.

Elsie: It takes a lot of time to stop feeling so empty. Even as I tell you this, I feel empty. But there are things that will ease it—first for a minute or two, then for a day or two. Then when you start letting good distractions of all kinds come into your life, you still know what's missing, but you don't feel as empty.

Eldred: It's amazing how much space my little wife took up in everybody's life. And it was so painful when I realized how empty and desolate everybody and everything was without her. Especially me and my whole life.

EnaMay: Where there was everything, there is now an empty hole of nothingness.

> *"Fragment. I am a fragment of us. I am a fragment composed of fragments." —Poet Rebecca Lindenberg*

* * *

E is for EUPHEMISMS

ME: Many people find "death" or "dead" very hard words to say, and they fear they may sound crass. You hear the following: expired, passed away, she's deceased, we lost him, went to be with God, in the arms of Jesus, gone, took her last sleep, untimely end, crossed the bar, succumbed to injuries, perished, and more. They're not wrong, per se, but you have your own reasons for the words you are OK with, and those you are not OK with. It's entirely up to you. But you must tell those around you what words you can handle.

Edna: There are three words that I couldn't stand hearing when our son died. The first one is that we "lost" him. We didn't misplace him. We didn't turn our backs and he ran away. He didn't wander into the bush. He died, and we could do nothing about it. We didn't cause it, we couldn't avoid it, we weren't careless, we didn't even know until we heard the words from the police officer. He at least said, "I'm sorry to have to tell you. Your son died." Ugly but true. Apparently, police know my brain had to hear that word so it could eventually understand what he was saying. "Lost" would mean we had to hurry and go with the police to find him. Then when somebody wrote, "Funeral services for the *late* …" I wanted to scream and tear up the paper and take the pieces back to the newspaper office and throw them on the floor and shout: His death wasn't "late." It was way too early. He was nineteen! That's not late in life. Late is what you are for work. Late is what you are for a meeting. What was he late for? NOTHING!

Ernie: Somebody who was afraid to use the words "died" or "death" with me actually used the word "expired" when asking about my wife. I have to believe she meant well, and the "D" words scared her, so she moved on to the next letter of the alphabet. E for "Expired." Your driver's license expires when you reach the limit and you have to renew it. I would give anything in this world to renew my time with my wife. Expiry dates are stamped on perishable foods. "Best before …" My wife wasn't past her best before date by any stretch of the imagination. A contract expires. Our marriage contract was forever. OK, it was "Til death do us part." And it expired only because she DIED.

Ella: It will probably sound a bit odd when I tell you that the words "beloved" and "his death must have been a surprise" made me cringe. Beloved is past tense. Love did not die with him. I will love him forever. He will always be alive in my heart and mind. As far as his death being a "surprise" because he seemed so healthy … well, that's just wrong. "Unexpected," yes. "Without warning," yes. But a surprise is what you get in the Cracker Jack box. It's a birthday party. It's a phone call from an old friend. It's something good. It makes you smile. But to me, a surprise is never this painful; it never brings on tears that never quit. And this "surprise" has never, ever shown me the prize.

Ed: I hated the word "died" and wanted people to use any word but that. It's so hard to hear when it's said with his name. "Deceased" is so much kinder somehow. And "went to be with Jesus" gives me some comfort.

* * *

Notes

F is for FEAR

Me: We're afraid of death. But the ensuing grief caused by a death creates an even deeper fear, because it's real in our minds. It's now in us, and it's a powerful force that can be debilitating to different degrees. We become afraid of many things now, including the future.

- I'm afraid because I don't know what to do right now or how to do it.
- I'm alone! How will I survive on my own?
- I'm afraid of the darkness inside and outside of me.
- I fear being alone in the present and the future. I fear having to rely on myself.
- I fear having to make all these decisions right now. What if I make the wrong one?
- I fear for my children and grandchildren.
- I'm suddenly afraid of strangers.
- I'm afraid because there are so many things I don't know.
- I fear any loud or unexpected noises.
- I was afraid I would have a nervous breakdown and be sent to a mental institute forever.
- I fear all the paperwork and the people who want it. My fear makes me nauseous.
- I'm afraid because ongoing fear is unfamiliar to me. I don't know how to stop it.
- I'm terrified something will happen to someone else I love—mostly my children and grandchildren.
- I fear doing anything, like driving, shopping, cooking, being alone, going into a crowd, and a thousand other things.

Me: I can tell you that with effort and help, each fear will be addressed by you down the road, and you will "slay the dragons" in your head. Find a trusted someone to talk to. Make a list of your fears and what you can do about them. Identifying them, putting them on paper, saying them out loud, and coming up with possible solutions helps you get control over them. They're real feelings, and they're difficult. But they can be tamed.

Florence: I was so afraid after her death, I couldn't breathe. I couldn't move. I couldn't sleep or eat. I had been so brave with her by my side, and now I was afraid of the entire nightmare I was in. I lay on the floor to feel a solidity under me. I held tightly to a polished rock to ground myself. I was comforted somewhat by people whose voices were just the right pitch and who spoke highly of my partner. As time went on, I learned my fears were bigger in my head than in reality. And I could handle them.

Frances: I became so tired of keeping my guard up because I had just learned that death can slam you in the face within seconds, no matter how vigilant you are. I had to keep moving, keep watching for the unexpected, or just go to sleep to get my mind off my fears of another death happening behind my back. There's no guarantee it won't happen again, but life helps you realize you can't keep being afraid.

* * *

F is for FORGIVENESS

Me: To forgive doesn't mean that you forget and suddenly spread love to the offender. To forgive is to cease to blame or feel resentment. It's something we can choose to do voluntarily for ourselves. We can let go of the thoughts of retaliation, of anger, and of resentment—feelings that have been weighing heavily on us and taking a huge toll on our minds, our bodies, and our spirits.

- I forgave, not because I could understand and accept what had happened and say it was OK, but because I needed to start my life over, without giving him any more of my time and energy.

- At first when she died, I was really angry at her. Apparently that's normal, but it didn't feel normal. She went away and left the kids and me alone. I thought about it a lot, and finally realized someone who loved us that much wouldn't die on purpose. She didn't intend to leave; she didn't choose to die. I forgave her. It sounds ridiculous, but I had to go through that before I could let go of the anger at her. I also realized that what I thought was anger was actually fear.
- The hardest thing I had to do for myself was to forgive. This didn't mean I wanted to start thinking what had happened was right, but because to heal my own mental health, I had to think less often of the guilty person and what she had done.

"You'll never know how strong your heart is until you learn to forgive who broke it." —unknown

"To forgive is to set a prisoner free and discover that the prisoner was you." —Lewis B. Smedes

"I think the first step is to understand that forgiveness does not exonerate the perpetrator. Forgiveness liberates the victim. It's a gift you give yourself." —T. D. Jakes

"It's not an easy journey to get to a place where you forgive people. But it is such a powerful place, because it frees you." —Tyler Perry

"When you hold resentment toward another, you are bound to that person or condition by an emotional link that is stronger than steel. Forgiveness is the only way to dissolve that link and get free." —Katherine Ponder

* * *

F is for FRIENDS

ME: My husband and I belonged to a Marriage Encounter (ME) group for thirty years. (No, it's not a swingers' group!) We would meet once a month for a potluck meal and to discuss anything that may affect our marriage, good or bad. We all became deep down friends. When my husband died suddenly, the ME group of eight was at my door before I got home. Their hugs helped me stand, and they did all the dirty work of phoning family and friends to tell them the bad news. I could hardly speak, let alone say my husband was dead. Then family that is blessedly also friends arrived. Another two very special friends showed up, and everybody helped with the immediate ugly stuff, then later did many things to help organize the Celebration of Life the way we wanted it: the music, the order of service, the photos, the branded urn, stories for the eulogy, the guest books, the food, the funeral card, choosing his many special things to be displayed on the tables that showed his incredible life, and on and on. Our daughter, through her own terrible grief, was the strong one who made many of the decisions with them. I'm still in this ME group of beautiful people God sent our way. And my daughter is still the strongest, yet softest friend I've been so fortunate to be blessed with.

Fern: A friend whose son had died about eighteen years earlier stood strongly by me. She never compared grief, and she never told me what to do. When I felt I was going insane, and had what we called "monkey mind," she stood by me. I had just met her when her son died, and our hearts melded. I was proud to stand by her. She reminded me that she grieved her loss her way, and I needed to grieve mine my way. But there were some things in common, one especially: listening. I had always called her my sister-of-the heart, and I couldn't believe she would worry about my pain when she had her own pain that never goes away. I can't begin to express to her how deeply she was a Godsend.

Fanny: My sister was my best friend through all of this. She stayed to help me cry and handed me my husband's pillow and hoodie to cry into. She helped me try to sort out my mind and the next necessary steps. She listened. She nodded. She did not say, "I understand," or "I know what you're going through," even though she probably did, better than anyone. She held my hand. She listened quietly in the night while I paced and cried. She helped me with the endless paperwork. She never told me what to do; she asked me what I wanted to do. She went home, but she phoned every other day, just to ask how my day went and what I did. She listened. She asked if there was anything I needed help with. Sometimes she just listened to me cry. Later she phoned about once a week when she felt I sounded better. Then she came to visit and went through everything with me again. That is profound love and support.

Fred: Friends couldn't stand to see me in such pain. They wanted to take it away, to fix me. They wanted me to be better, and neither they nor I knew how to make that happen. So they said encouraging things and told me they were thinking of me. This death was something horrible and new for everybody to deal with, but I knew they would be there for me at all hours of the day and night.

Felicity: Two friends of mine did everything for me at first. Everything. My mail, my groceries, my cleaning, my cooking, my laundry. And pretty soon I believed I couldn't do it myself. I became selfish with their time. And one day when they didn't show up, I had to admit that I was disappointed, and even a bit angry. After I got up, made coffee, made and ate my toast, and did the dishes, I realized I was not doing our friendship any favor. I needed them. But it was to hold my hand, talk to me, let me cry, give me hugs, then return to their own families. We discussed it and they agreed it was time to let me do my own things around the house, but they would be there for things of the mind and heart.

Farley: Most of the people who showed up at the funeral weren't even our friends. They were what I call "lookey-lou snoops," as in our small town everybody comes to everybody's funeral. Three of my lifelong buddies and their wives were there, and really, they were the only ones I could handle seeing or talking to. I watched some of the pretend friends as they ate my food and went their own way. I didn't tell them, but I thought, *They can kiss my ass. My wife was a tremendous person, but she wasn't good enough for some of them when she was alive, so they sure as hell can't pretend she's good enough for them now that she's dead.* Bitter? No. Just realistic. My buddies and their wives loved her, and they can continue to take me fishing and hunting, laugh or be sad with me, and to have a beer with me. That's all I need for good friends.

"The first to help you up are the ones who know how it feels to fall down." —unknown

"When friendship leaves us through death, we feel cheated in life. Life doesn't play fair, so I vow to win the game for us both." —Amy Hoover

* * *

F is for F***

Me: There are many swear words that get bandied about with grief. F*** was my favorite from the start. My husband was hit by a tree, and it immediately became "that f***ing tree." F*** can be used as a noun, a verb, an adjective, an adverb, a good old expletive, and in other creative ways. People tell me they have used it in anger and rage, sadness, loneliness, helplessness, hate, bitterness, and for many other reasons while grieving. There's a small satisfaction in the word. The word is offensive to some, but please don't judge. Just skip this.

Fran: I had never used that word before, but it felt good to shout it out, and I did it often. I also used other swear words and realized it was the only thing at that moment I had any control over. So I used it with purpose (and with no real purpose) to swear in anger. I felt like it came from my soul.

Finley: I was in bed by myself, and I punched my pillow and said, "F***!" I needed to get rid of some anger, so I did that another twenty or twenty-five times, and even smiled through my tears because nobody would believe I was saying that word each time. I did that often. It helped.

Fargo: I normally swear, but I had never used that word so much in my life as when my brother was killed. I was so angry and heartbroken. My wife finally nicely reminded me there were other swear words I could use, or maybe I could actually use it a little less. I think I did switch to other words. Somewhat. No f***ing apologies from me!

Freidrich: I actually couldn't think of any other words when the police told me my wife died, so I just kept repeating, "F***." Then I put it in every question I asked them. They didn't care. They were real good about how I was acting.

Felix: I'm a good Christian, and as long as you're not using my real name, I have to admit I used that unfamiliar word at least half a dozen times, and it felt good. It felt like a sin, and I was angry at God, so I shouted it. I wasn't using the Lord's name in vain, though, so what the heck.

Flynn: The day my good friend was killed a lot of swear words and phrases flitted somewhere in my head and then were swept away, like dandelion fluff. The only word that stayed was "F***!" It felt appropriate.

Faith: You don't know what a big mess you are until a rude person feels the need to remind you. You're doing what you can, you're breathing, and you're getting groceries when he asks you how you are. I say, "Honestly? I'm not doing too good." And he says "Yeah, I'm sorry you're still a mess." So I say, "F*** you," and it's bad, but it feels good.

* * *

F is for FUNERALS

Me: A funeral is to mark a death, a ceremony for family and friends to gather together to honor the life that he or she shared while on earth. But you're not obligated to have one. The only thing that's mandatory is that you dispose of the body in a legal manner, and you must register the death.

It can be many things:

- It can be public or private, a full funeral arranged by a funeral home, a simple memorial service, a Celebration of Life, or nothing at all.
- It can be inside a building, or on a mountaintop, or any point in between.
- It can be a burial or a cremation.

- Some forward-thinking people have planned (or even paid for) their funerals/memorials/celebrations ahead of time and given the information to several people so nobody has to guess what's wanted.
- The toughest thing is this: You're being asked to make decisions on how you want to dispose of your loved one's dead body, when all you want in this world is to have the live, warm body back.

Frank: I actually hate funerals when the body is there. Ashes are OK, but a body stresses me. I'm OK with memorials or celebrations, because people know it's OK to cry, but it's more important to laugh and share some great memories too. It's better when there's lots of photos displayed and you can see things that were important to that person. And you have to have good food, especially open-face egg salad buns. It's not a good send-off without them. Forget the flowers. Do donations to non-profits instead. Just bring yourself and your stories.

Faith: This is odd, but I figured out the total cost of sympathy cards I received, and it was over $800. It would be better if people just signed a piece of paper with a nice message on it and enclosed it with a donation to a non-profit in the family's name.

Fay: It may not be standard practice, but we took our seven- and nine-year-old children to their eleven-year-old cousin's funeral. He was killed in a quad roll-over, and I heard them asking each other if they thought he was "smashed up" or whether there was "blood all over" or even whether his "guts spilled out." We realized their imaginations were scaring them worse than reality, and we knew their cousin had no facial injuries. We discussed the death and the upcoming funeral with them honestly and succinctly. I'm glad we took them, as it led to appropriate discussion about death that they had been worried and curious about. But *PREPARE THEM* for what they will see and hear and all the tears they will encounter. If you need help to deal with them, get a package from the funeral home or library or mental health office. And listen, listen to everything your children say.

Flora: I tell you from experience working funerals for many years: the celebration can be a thing of beauty or a day of problems if not thought out ahead of time. I've helped with a lot of funerals and have seen a lot of tricky challenges. Where do the ex-spouse and family sit? What happens when there are family members who hate each other? Somebody feels a recent boyfriend of girlfriend should be included as family in the obituary and in the introductions, and others are totally against it? What about when people who aren't asked to speak insist on picking up the mic to speak or sing? What about a fight over who gets reserved parking? Or the eulogy is terrible, inappropriate, or doesn't include anything about the full life of the deceased? Or you can't hear the eulogy because a toddler is crying at the top of her lungs? Or the minister hardly mentions the deceased's name? If some estranged family members want a big doggie bag when they leave the luncheon, what then? Somebody wants alcohol served, others don't? I'm sure there are hundreds of other challenging funeral stories. These are just a few of mine. It's a shame everybody can't agree to do what's right for the deceased loved one, but no, some can't. Thank goodness the day will eventually be over—not always, but usually—without fisticuffs!

Fergus: I didn't feel that I was there at all. I let myself be somewhere else in my mind while people were talking. Same at the luncheon. I removed myself in my mind while people were greeting me. Somehow I thought it would protect me so I wouldn't cry. Really, it just made me feel stupid and blank after I left. And I would have had support for my tears.

> *"A well-loved local character wrote the following seating instructions for his funeral: family, friends and Oiler's fans at the front; Flame's fans at the back; and Leaf's fans, don't even bother coming."* —Harold Hansen, from his obituary

> *"Sitting at your funeral, my mind knows that you are gone, but my heart will never accept it."* —Margaret Thibault

> *"When I was greeting people at the funeral, my mouth kept saying, 'I'm OK.' Or 'I'm fine.' But my heart kept saying, 'I'm broken. I'm not OK.'"* —Margaret Thibault

> *"One of the hardest lessons in life is letting go."* —Mareez Reyes

> *"Even the best of friends cannot attend each other's funeral."* —Kehlog Albran

* * *

Notes

G is for GOODBYE ...
and GOODBYE ... and GOODBYE

Me: Dementia, and especially Alzheimer's, rate right up there with the cruelest of illnesses. The person you love is physically there, but they're no longer living the life you once knew, so neither are you. They become a total stranger. How many goodbyes do you have to live through? There is no answer.

I've been told you lose your loved one four times: When he is diagnosed. When he goes through the different stages of loss. When he goes into care. And when he physically dies.

There's a constant mid-level angry grief when watching the mind and spirit of a loved one regress and disappear slowly while his or her body stays within sight. When do you say goodbye to his mind? His brain is dying in pieces. How often do you grieve another of his losses: memory, sense of humor, thoughts and ideas, beloved hobbies, mental abilities, physical abilities, bodily functions? It's the longest goodbye anyone can experience.

With the frustration and anger at what's happening to a beautiful human, there is also guilt. Human guilt at not being able to fix things, and for getting angry and hating what's happening. This is normal guilt that hopefully each person can move beyond. Remember: YOU ARE HUMAN. The situation is abnormal. Some people say carrying an old photo helps to fiercely hang on to the love they still hold deep inside.

Gwen: I thought the worst had happened when my mother was diagnosed with dementia. But as I watched Mom slip away and be replaced by a physically present stranger, every day was a goodbye. As she went through different stages, I lost parts of her. When she went into care, I lost a big part of her.

I visited regularly. Even when she whined "Shut up! Who are you? Get out!" I continued my visits. I realized the cruel words actually came from "the stranger." And then there were no words.

When did I first realize the mom I knew had passed into nowhere land? When she couldn't answer simple questions? Goodbye, intelligent Mom. The first time she didn't recognize me? Goodbye, loving Mama Bear Mom, my fiercest cheerleader. When she accused me of stealing money, jewelry, and candy from her night stand? Goodbye, generous and kind Mom. When she sat hunched in her wheelchair, not even lifting her head, as I gently whispered to her? Goodbye, strong, dignified, classy and athletic Mom. And it seemed each day a little more was snatched from her. Goodbye, my loving Mom.

Is there a halfway point to Heaven where a person's soul sits, waiting for the body to give up? This breathing stranger was propped up in what was once my mom's life. I daily cried and grieved the loss of my "real" mom in little ways and big ways. It's a total fallacy that we grieve only at physical death.

Thank God for the beautiful eulogy Mom's sister gifted us with. Mom again became the bright-eyed woman full of joy, the athlete, the dancer, the caring and loving wife, mother, and grandmother, the generous community-minded person who loved to laugh. For a few minutes, I had my "real" mom back. But what guests that day didn't know was I had no more goodbyes left. I had only a heartfelt wish for my precious mom's mind to catch up to her spirit in the place beyond.

Gil: I couldn't go visit my mom and see her deteriorate into a helpless being, so I hardly ever went to see her. At first she would cry for me to take her to the farm with her mom and dad. They were long dead. I couldn't change anything, and I couldn't deal with it. I stopped in about once a month. I felt guilty because I couldn't watch this slow and undignified dying. It was awful, especially when she got to the point where there was nothing left but a drooling stranger. I tell myself my real mom would understand and forgive me for being such a coward. But I don't think I've forgiven myself. I just couldn't say goodbye a hundred times over to a stranger.

Gary: God, I loved the person my wife was through our marriage, but I didn't know how to love who she became with Alzheimer's. I hated myself because there was a brief point one day where I wanted to shake her and shout at her to stop letting herself go downhill, almost like she could "get over it." How terrible was I? And the guilt of those thoughts brought me to my knees and left me so critically angry at myself and the world that I couldn't sleep. I tried to calm myself by thinking, *This is my job. I have loved her for forty-nine years.* I meant it when I swore that I would love her "through sickness and health, for better or worse." But I didn't want to say goodbye to anything that she was losing to the disease, because I was losing her in the process. Thankfully, the wonderful nurses and caregivers stepped in and convinced me it was not my job to "do" or fix the unfixable, but just to "be" with her. They also convinced me they are well trained to meet my wife's needs and helped me take the time to identify and say goodbye to the many things that were already gone. Then I was able to visit her with a bit more patience, a better understanding, and not as much guilt. (I feel it's important that you know I never shook my wife in our entire time together. That's what made my thoughts even more dishonorable.)

* * *

G is for GRATITUDE

Me: It's so important for our mental health to identify and appreciate the gratitude we feel along the way. It's not easy at first, because you may feel there's nothing to be grateful for. He's dead, and you hurt, and life is not fair. But eventually I realized there were things I was grateful for regarding my husband's death: it was sudden; he was in a place that he loved, doing what he loved; our children and grandchildren were not there that day to witness it; and the RCMP who responded treated everyone with dignity and respect.

Stop and make a list of what you're grateful for. This is what I was very grateful for:

- The forty-five wonderful years we so enjoyed together and the memories of them. In particular, I was so grateful for the family we produced together: our son and our daughter, son-in-law, and three incredible grandchildren who filled our life with love.

- Our friends and families. We were blessed with the best. My husband's siblings all flew to Alberta from Ontario and Quebec for the Celebration of Life, for which I am full of gratitude. My family showed up immediately from all over Alberta to be with our family. I am thankful to this day when I hear their voices on the phone. I am so thankful for my sister and brother-in-law who have walked beside me every day since the death.
- The speakers who shared such special words at the Celebration of Life, and the friends and family from near and far who honored him by attending, leaving cards and donating in his memory to a cause close to our hearts—the Fallen Four Memorial Park.
- The RCMP who honored him with Red Serge.
- The funeral guidance and the spiritual guidance.
- The hundreds of photos that bring back thousands of great memories. They show life and love and enjoyment and action. It's special times of him alone, with family, with friends, relatives, his animals, strangers, and mentors. And I'm grateful for the videos, where for precious moments I can see him breathing and moving.
- Being able to show and accept love.
- The sun, the moon, and the stars that are a presence no matter what I do with my day and night.
- For my niece who has helped me meditate and develop my spiritual connections.
- This list could go on for many, many pages. My gratitude lifts my spirits immensely.

When you need positive reinforcement, stop and make a list of what you're grateful for. Stop and give thanks every day. Say it out loud. It doesn't solve every problem, but it does help mitigate the pain.

"I have not heard your voice in years, but my heart has conversations with you every day." —allgreatquotes.com

* * *

G is for GRIEF IS LIKE ...

Me: The dictionary says grief is a deep and intense sorrow, a keen mental suffering over affliction or loss. Actually, grief is like nothing you can fully describe, but different people say this:

- Grief is like waking up after being severely beaten and trying to figure out why and where you have damage, and what to do about it.
- Grief is like trying to walk while weighted down in tight concrete shoes, and it hurts, and your legs won't work, and you always feel like you're going to fall, and none of this makes sense.
- Grief is like an earthquake or a tornado or some natural disaster. It sweeps in quickly, you have no control, you see the fallout, but it doesn't make sense, and the devastation is long-lasting. It's a long time before the ground feels safe under you again.
- Grief is like waves on the ocean. Sometimes you feel yourself slogging along the shore, tripping in the deep sand, often falling. The tide comes in and the waves knock you off your feet. You panic and can't breathe. You flail around stupidly, feeling darkness close in on you, unable to breathe, fighting the water. You thought you were a strong swimmer, but you don't know how to save yourself. Part of you hits the sand again, and you're able to drag yourself onto a bit more solid ground. And the tide goes out. But when you turn your back, the tide rushes in and knocks you down again.
- Grief is like being dropped in a strange country alone. Nobody can understand your language, and you have no map. You move, but the roads and streets are a jumble with sharp turns everywhere. You're in very unfamiliar territory, and you don't know how to ask anyone anything, or where to turn.
- Grief is like walking around naked with your heart on the wrong side of your ribs. Everything's just hangin' out there.
- Grief is like looking at a beautiful garden through a window when, suddenly, someone shatters the window. The beautiful garden is still there, but what you see is totally distorted by the cracks in the glass. Everything looks and feels broken, and your life is shattered.

- Grief is like being in a big balloon, away from the world you knew, even though you can see it through a fog. Nobody around you can understand where you've gone, what you need, or what you're doing. They all wonder when you will come out into their world again. They don't know yet that you will never join the old world in the same way.
- Grief is like a movie channel that goes off. Normal service will resume when the pain is fixed. We lost the original life story but will continue with a movie that may contain scenes of anger, fear, and a plot that's difficult to follow. Rest assured we will return to the release of the never-ending new life story when it's ready. We're still working on it. —Margaret Thibault

> *"Grief, I've learned is really just love. It's all the love you want to give, but cannot. All that unspent love gathers up in the corners of your eyes, the lump in your throat and in that hollow part of your chest. Grief is just love with no place to go."* —Jamie Anderson

> *"Grief is a fulcrum. The joint in time between the vanishing of hope and the beginning of loss."* —Ann-Marie MacDonald, <u>The Way the Crow Flies</u>,

> *"No one ever told me that grief felt so much like fear."* —C.S. Lewis

> *(Grief makes you feel)* *"... penitent, true isolation even in a crowd, a dull fury, bewildered, overwhelmed, no one in the universe understands so you're left floating in unfamiliar air, like looking out an airplane window and wondering if that's a scene from up high or just before landing."* —David Adams Richards, <u>Mercy Among the Children</u>

> *"Grief is like being handed a role in a play with no script. At your first appearance, your body goes numb and your mind goes blank. You don't know the words or the plot, and you start to panic, especially when you realize it's*

*your reality and you can't just walk off stage and go
home. It becomes your role."—Margaret Thibault*

* * *

G is for GUILT

Me: There are many reasons people feel guilt when someone dies. Anxiety and guilt wear us down to an exhausted shell of our old self. We feel relief when a loved one dies after suffering. Then we feel ... you got it ... GUILT. In most situations, guilt is normal. We can wear the cloak of guilt if we want, but somewhere along the line that cloak gets too heavy and needs removed so we can grieve openly.

Gail: I'm sure my friend was beyond suffering from advanced dementia. I tried to use telepathy to give her a quiet message to settle her head in her pillow and take her last breath. And every time, I felt guilty for wishing this. We'd all watched her decline from a vivacious matriarch to a seemingly vacant shell. We all believed that who she was no longer lived inside this horrible prison of dementia, and her spirit had moved to another realm. Even though I knew she would never choose to continue like this, I felt guilty every time I said, "My beautiful friend, it's OK to let go and follow your spirit."

Gloria: For over three years my husband had threatened suicide, but he wouldn't tell me where, when, or how. And he refused help. Every morning I would wake up and be stressed, wondering if this was the day. I got worn down from worry, helplessness, lack of sleep, and anger. Secretly I got where I felt it would be easier to deal with his death than the anxiety of being scared. I felt guilty for my thoughts. One day I did find him dead. Ironically, he died of a heart attack. It was such a weight off my shoulders. Of course, I felt terribly guilty about that. I couldn't tell anybody until now.

Garth: I don't think I will ever feel guilt like I did when I said they could unplug the machines that were keeping my wife alive. She had suffered a stroke and was in a deep coma. I took the last few moments to thank her for our precious love and for all the beauty and cherished memories she had given the kids, grandkids, and me in our great life together, and I was honoring her wish to have her organs donated. I was repeating what I had already said a hundred times, but I was prolonging the moment I knew was coming. And now I still question my decision. The guilt is still there because I was the one who said, "Yes," even though the family and I had all agreed with the doctors and nurses. It was right. For her, not me.

Gordon: The time I spent in prison helped me come to terms with the guilt of having been the driver when my best friend was killed. The worst of it is remembering exactly when I made the fateful decision to drive drunk. I grabbed the keys from him when we left the party and said, "I'll show you what your hot rod can *really* do." Yeah, I really showed him. He's dead. And I am the guilty drunk driver.

Georgine: My adult children did most of the hard stuff getting ready for their dad's funeral. They were protecting me, which later made me feel so guilty. A mother is supposed to protect her children. I finally got it together enough that I could help *them*. It helped with the guilt to share ideas and jobs, cry together, and share memories. But I also felt guilty that I hadn't been there for them the first day their dad died, as I was too wrapped up in my own shock and grief. My incredible children lectured me on how sometimes a role reversal is totally acceptable. We're getting through it together, but I still feel guilt every once in a while. I just try not to tell them anymore.

Glenys: You cannot imagine the guilt when you have accidentally killed a child with your vehicle. I wanted the police to charge me and take me to jail forever. They thoroughly investigated the facts and tried to reassure me that it was definitely not my fault. But that doesn't mean I didn't feel horribly guilty. I couldn't sleep, and thought I should never have children, as I didn't deserve any. It took quite a while with a psychiatrist to help me work on this. Finally, I can say my guilt and anxiety do not dictate my life.

* * *

Notes

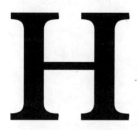

H is for HEALING

Me: Your healing is occurring alongside everything you do, say, and think. Every day, whether you realize it or not. You will always have scars, but they will remind you of how far you've come from the initial pain. Life has a way of bringing us people, busy-ness, purpose, information, light, nature, and other positive distractions to bring us through the dark. Some will be in front, some beside, some behind, and some above you. And most importantly, the person working the hardest at healing is you.

Me: For those grieving the loss of a child, I just want to say that I firmly believe there is an invisible golden cord still connecting mother and child. The umbilical cord is cut at birth, but I believe the golden cord can never be severed. And maybe at moments that is all you have to hang on to in the process of healing.

There are ways of survival that you develop while you are healing that will:

- help you find how strong your spirit is.
- help you try to make the best of the worst. And you will.
- help you rest without quitting.
- help you move from being in pieces to being somewhat at peace.
- help you breathe when that's all you can do that day.
- help you connect to your life.
- help you rebuild the protective barriers that death knocked down.
- help you eventually find small moments of acceptance and even soft contentment.
- help you realize grief is a passage, not a place to stay.

Everything about nature, writing, music and songs, dancing, rhythm, painting, reading, just thinking, praying, and going to church, hobbies, photo albums, planning, and setting goals—there are hundreds more "ways" of healing for hundreds more people. What's yours?

- We fall. We break. We rise. We fall. We break. We rise. But after a while, when we rise, we begin looking for ways to heal, and we overcome.
- I made a choice. Grief is here, but it's not my identity. Defeat is here, but it's just resting for a moment. I will drive it out by finding ways to rise above it and heal.

When life puts you through a tumbler, it's your choice whether you come out polished or crushed.—Elisabeth Kubler-Ross

"When you start doubting yourself, remember how far you have come. Remember everything you have faced, all the battles you have won. And all the fears you have overcome." — Idillire — means idyllic in Afrikaan, from Facebook Quotes and Sayings

"What we have once enjoyed deeply we can never lose. All that we love deeply become a part of us." —Helen Keller.

"I do not want the peace which passeth understanding; I want the understanding that bringeth peace."—Helen Keller

"Let the winds of creation cleanse this bogged down mind." —Rupert Schmitt

* * *

H is for HEARTBEAT

Me: It used to be when the sun went down, my heartbeat and my energy level went up. I also loved to be scared by a ride at the fair, or by a movie, because my heart would pound in my chest, and I'd say: "Wow, that was fun!" I knew it wasn't real, or ongoing.

But the fallout from our four RCMP officers being shot and killed on March 3, 2005 was real, ongoing, and terrifying. It was 3:00 a.m., and I was walking to our door. I really needed my husband, my rock.

As I walked, I looked up at the stars. I put my hand up to the side of my neck and accidentally felt my heartbeat. Thump-thump. Thump-thump. I suddenly felt the calm in that sound and saw the face of my sister. Thump-thump. Another sister. Thump-thump. Another sister. Thump-thump. A friend. With the beats of my heart, a strong loved one took his or her place in my mind and left a glow. A star. A message. They were all there—a parade of strength. I wasn't even close to being alone.

I looked up. The stars were shining brightly in this huge universe. I looked at the door. I knew my strong husband was waiting for me in this night and was only a heartbeat away.

Me: When my husband died, my heart would go on overdrive in my chest, banging against my ribs and making me dizzy. Then it would be quiet, and I wasn't sure—and didn't care—if it was beating. After about a week, I remembered to lift my hand to my heartbeat and wait for the reminder of the beautiful faces of support to appear in my mind. Their hearts are beating with mine. Try it. It works and is incredibly calming. There's a constant calming echo of my husband in my thoughts but especially in my heartbeat.

Helen: Of course, I've never had my heart literally ripped out of my chest. But I think grief is what it feels like when someone reaches below the ribs, cups that vital organ in two hands, and pulls. Everybody I've talked to has said it hurts like a sonofabitch, and they're right. My husband's heart stopped beating, and mine was suddenly over-beating, raging, knocking against my ribs, pumping forcefully in my ears and my throat. I felt the need to throw up, but I was afraid my heart would fly out of my mouth.

Harley: So often I could hear the loud swish of my heartbeat in my ears as the blood kept rushing to my head. That's all I could hear sometimes. Was it to remind me I was still alive? For a while it just reminded me that my workaholic husband had no heartbeat anymore, and all the money we'd made was for nothing. Then it made me think he wanted me to do something from the heart. Now I sit in an arena named for him that we helped build. I hear the swish of skates in my ears as the heartbeats of the young athletes carry them across the ice.

"In the stillness of the quiet, if we listen, we can hear the whisper of the heart giving strength to weakness; courage to fear; hope to despair." —Howard Thurman

"To live in the hearts we leave behind is not to die." —Thomas Campbell

This incredible story was on Facebook: A young man's organs had been donated when he was killed. The family who was blessed with his heart for their loved one knew the young donor's family would be devastated with their loss. They recorded their healed family member's new transplanted heartbeat, bought a bear from Build-a-Bear, and had the heartbeat recording put in it. They gave it to the family of the deceased young man, and now his family can hold the bear and hear their dead son's heartbeat once more. What an amazing gift for all.

* * *

H is for HEREAFTER

Me: The pain of my husband's death will never completely leave, but it helped me a bit to look at death somewhat differently. Being born leads to living here on earth, and dying leads to being born in a new place. Never mind whether you believe in Heaven or hell, or saints and sinners. I have to believe there is a new world my husband was born into at death, and that it's good, or I wouldn't be able to let him go. The hereafter is my stronghold.

For those who watched the slow death of someone with dementia, please take a moment and read on. When you're born, you're in a fetal position. You're received into the wide-open arms of your excited mom and dad. You breathe, you cry. You're introduced to this new world and your new life.

You slowly unfurl from your fetal position. You're put in a room where other people decide where you will sleep, what you will eat, and what things of interest you might like around you. You see fuzzy faces, but you don't know what smiling and talking mean. And you look out the window from which you have a limited glimpse of the world. You say your first words. You take your first cautious steps. You cry for food, or a diaper change, or you're tired, or you have gas, or something hurts, or you need attention. You learn to speak. You learn to run. You're on your way to a greatly expanded world.

Now watch a person who is dying and failing in health physically or mentally or both. They no longer move with purpose but with caution. Then they stop walking, and they stop talking. When they lose their language, they cry and make unusual sounds, asking for the same things they did as a baby: they need food, or a diaper change, or they're tired, or they have gas, or something hurts, or they need attention. They're in a room decided by others and lie in a bed decided by others. The things in the room are things someone has decided the person likes around them. They see new fuzzy faces, but they no longer seem to know or care what smiling and talking mean. They see out the window, but they have a limited glimpse of the world.

And they lie small in the bed, lastly curling into a fetal position on their way through death to be born in a greatly under-rated new world beyond. Can you see them being welcomed with open arms once more?

* * *

H is for HOPE

Me: There is ALWAYS hope. When you give up hope, you have nothing. You say, "I hope …" many times without realizing it. It can be for small things or big things, but I wouldn't recommend hoping for the impossible. In grief, it's important to welcome hope into your heart and spirit for your survival. To pray is to have hope that you will be guided and comforted. Hope is believing or trusting there is something more positive in life than this moment, this day, this situation.

- I have a candleholder that says: "Perhaps they are not stars, but rather openings in Heaven where the love of our lost ones pours through and shines down upon us to let us know they are happy." That reinforces my hope every day.
- In grief, the road ahead seems endlessly fraught with twists and turns, switchbacks, detours, and bad conditions. But it's only a small part of life's journey. We eventually come back to the manageable and smoother highway that gives us hope. Remember that as you move on, a better life is part of that ongoing hope, not a destination you suddenly arrive at.
- I encourage you to have hope and not be pulled under by your broken world. All broken things can be mended. Not only with time, as they say, but with intention. Hope with intention. Look for hope in the darkness where you shine your flickering light. Move on with intention.

"Hope is not the conviction that something will turn out well, but the certainty that something makes sense, regardless of how it turns out." —Vaclav Havel

"Once you choose hope, anything is possible."
—Christopher Reeve

"We are meant to live in joy. This does not mean that life will be easy or painless. It means that we can turn our

faces to the wind and accept that this is the storm we must pass through." —*Archbishop Desmond Tutu*

* * *

H is for HOW ARE YOU?

Me: This question is asked automatically by the general public as a courtesy to everybody, including the bereaved: "How are you?" It's an automatic question that in grief there is not really an answer to, other than one honest word: shitty, terrified, lonely, shocked, confused, overwhelmed, angry, hopeless, helpless, and so on. But we're not usually in the mood to continue the conversation, or embarrass the person asking, so we usually answer with what we know is a lie: "I'm OK." And we move on. We're not OK: we're not even close to OK, and we know our feelings may change to worse over the next minute, hour, or day. But they're hard feelings we don't want to, or may not be able to, discuss.

There is no perfect answer, but there are suggestions (Maybe follow them with "Thanks for asking. I need to get home.):

- I'm as good as I can be, considering.
- I'm looking for magic.
- I'm just living on memories for now.
- I'm living the nightmare.
- I will get through this and be OK someday.
- I'm breathing. That's the best I can say for now.
- I don't really know. But thanks for asking.
- I'm still off balance. But I'm putting one foot in front of the other.
- I'm very grateful for the family and friends I have.
- I haven't found the words to describe an answer to that question.
- I'm struggling. But I'm trying.
- I'm workin' on it.
- Please ask me that in a year.
- Today is not a good day to ask me that.

- I'm in another world right now.
- I'm just trying my best to get through this (grocery shopping, banking, getting the mail, etc.).

And my favorite that I use regularly: "I'm OK until I'm not OK." There are many others, but it's up to you to decide your own, and don't hesitate to use it.

* * *

H is for HOW MANY CHILDREN DO YOU HAVE?

Me: To lose a child is beyond my capacity to imagine. Like many others, I can't go there. But you, or someone you know, has been through that hell. And one of the difficult questions you may be asked is, "How many children do you have?" How you answer is totally what *you* have come up with.

Heather: After our son died, new acquaintances would ask how many children we have. I would say three and change the subject. I don't think I owe it to anyone who doesn't know the story to explain we have two children on earth and one in Heaven. He lives in my heart, so we really do still have three children. My husband thinks we should start saying out loud: "Two children on earth and one in Heaven." I might someday, when I can say it without bursting into tears.

Hadrian: After our newborn baby died of complications, and people asked how many children we had, I would point to our two-year-old daughter and say, "We have this beautiful little girl, and she has an angel sister in Heaven."

Hal: For a short time, I didn't know what to say, so I would say the new number, as we still have four. And I always felt guilty. So in honor of my son, I found the courage to say, "We were very fortunate to have five wonderful children for twenty-two years, and now we have four. How about you?"

* * *

Notes

 is for IN BETWEEN

Me: You have to be paying attention, but there is a moment when all pain goes away. When your mind forgets. When your heart beats happily. Nobody is dead.

It's only for a split second. It's right when you're waking and walking the fine line between sleep and reality. For just an instant, you feel normal. Not hollowed out, but full. The softness of the sheets caresses you, and the pillow holds you gently. Cherish that fleeting moment.

And then you open your eyes and everything crashes back on top of you and into you. You realize nothing has changed, but you slept some.

Know there will eventually come a day you will wake and see light, and the crash won't be as hard, and some softness will stay.

* * *

I is for INTIMACY LOST

Me: People think of intimacy as purely sex. Great stuff, but, for many of us, intimacy is so much more than quick sex or making slow love, and we miss it all. It was:

- texting in the middle of the day just to say "I love you" or "Waiting for you" or just an emoji heart.
- phoning and saying, "I love you," followed by sweet nothings and "I miss you."
- cards and notes signed a certain way.

- holding hands, or his hand on my neck, back, or bum, touching each other just for the solidity of the action.
- our eyes meeting across the room and knowing what the other one was thinking.
- snuggling up to watch a movie or to read together.
- being anxious to leave a public event to get home for private time.
- laughingly feeding each other grapes because we'd seen it in an old movie.
- talking dirty just for the fun of it.
- hugs for all reasons and for no reasons.
- laughing together about what happened during the day, or something from the past that only we shared and would understand.
- secret words or signals that cracked us up.
- writing love messages and hiding them in his suitcase, one for each day he was away.
- watching each other dress and undress.
- dancing close together, whether at a dance or at home.
- kissing to say "Glad you're home" or "See you later" or just for the fun of it.
- whispering secrets.
- Marriage Encounter sharing time, and discussion or action when we got home.
- pet names for each other.
- touching skin to skin through the night and reaching out for one another if we strayed too far apart in the bed.

Many things were intimate just because they were shared with love. And now, heart-breakingly, that's gone. My ears, eyes, hands, all my skin, my heart, my toes, all my body, my mind, and my feelings miss everything about my husband so much, so many times a day.

Anyone learning to live without a partner who has died recognizes many of these and other intimacies precious to you.

Irene: When my husband died, my night-time dreams were crazy. They were about sexual intimacies in every house we had lived in. We moved six times in our marriage, and every house had a reminder of great sex. I had occasionally thought of it with a smile, but now I was dreaming about it all in vivid detail. I always woke up so sad and lonely. And forgive my bluntness, but horny as hell.

Single people, don't tell me you didn't become a DIY person like me when it comes to sex. It's certainly not the same, but it's the best any of us can do.

Isaac: We weren't intimate, really. We loved each other, sure. But for the last twenty years or so, we had separate beds, because I snored so bad. I was used to sleeping in my own bed. Occasionally we would have sex, but we chose to share other intimate moments, and that's what I have lost.

* * *

I is for ISOLATION

Me: *Ongoing isolation for any length of time is not good for your mental health. If you find yourself socially isolated and depressed, it's time to seek professional help.* However, isolation for a few hours in the middle of the chaos is a way to rest your mind and body. Totally alone time to look at your grief. You don't have to pretend anything for anybody. Or try to make conversation. Or try to follow another person's conversations. Or try to be a hostess. Or eat and drink because somebody brought you something. Isolation can be in a rocking chair, a room, a bed, or outside—anywhere you can isolate from others. Take this time to drop your shoulders and breathe deeply, gather and re-sort thoughts, cry, and talk to the loved one who isn't here but who has hijacked every moment of your mind. It's easier to breathe and talk to the next world in isolation. But it's very important to return to friends and family.

Ike: You might call it isolation, but I call it healing. I went to my cabin after the funeral and didn't come out for over a month. I kept in touch with one friend every couple of days, so he could tell people not to worry about me. But I fished or just sat quietly in my boat on the water, thinking. I chopped wood to relieve the anger and frustration. I read westerns, as it was easy to follow the plot. I sat by my fireplace and watched the flames for half the night. I talked lots, but it was to myself, my deceased wife, and Mother Nature. I wanted the isolation. I had to sort this out by myself before I could be with anybody else. I still do that sometimes to get my head on straight. It's my healing.

Isobelle: When my husband died suddenly, I was terrified of isolation. I lived on a farm nineteen miles from the nearest town and six miles from the nearest neighbor. We thought the isolation was great when we got married and raised our children out there. We had each other. The kids grew up and moved on. None of them wanted to live on the old farm that far out of town. When my partner died, he took my courage with him. To alleviate my fears, I put the farm up for sale. I actually lived in terror of my own shadow and every sound I heard in the night until it sold. I didn't have anybody to talk to about it. It wasn't mentally healthy. When I moved to town, I put double locks on every door and was just regularly afraid, not terrified, of my future without him. But now I see my family more often, I got mental health help, and I have other people to talk to and socialize with, so I'm doing much better.

* * *

Notes

J

is for JEALOUSY

Me: Don't be surprised if you're jealous that someone else—friend, family, or stranger—still has their spouse, child, parent, friend, or other loved one. You're not a bad person. You're human. And you're having to get used to your loss. It's part of the yearning part of grief. You are unintentionally reminded of what you no longer have. It eventually gets better when you talk about it.

Jerry: I struggled to be around my teenage nieces after my daughter died. They were so full of life and had been good friends with Janice. I knew it was selfish, but I was so jealous of my sisters, as they still had their daughters. I made excuses for not visiting, but my sisters soon caught on. They were grieving too, but they understood. And my nieces actually talked to me about *their* grief and about my daughter's life and death, and we cried and laughed together, which made a world of difference.

Joannie: When I had my miscarriage, it seemed every second woman I saw on the street was pregnant. I was so jealous. And two different friends announced their pregnancies the week after I discovered my little bud baby had died. Then there was a baby shower. Again, I was so jealous. I tried hard to be happy for everyone, and I was. It's just that when I got home, I would cry and grieve our baby that hadn't grown to birth. I don't think people understand how important it is to grieve a miscarriage. It's a death of many dreams.

Jackie: When my mom died, believe it or not, I was jealous of my friend's mom. Mother and daughter were so close. Mom and I hadn't been as close, but I was still jealous of the life they got to continue sharing. My friend's mom understood and slowly took me under her wing, not as a daughter, but as a friend who needed someone. She helped me be happy for the two of them and for the good memories I did have with Mom.

Jill: My husband and I were real loners, and his funeral was very small. I was OK with that at the time. When my friend's husband died, I was jealous of the number of people who showed up to celebrate his life. That's just strange ... to compare and be jealous of the number of mourners at a funeral.

Jerod: Nothing tore our family of three apart as much as jealousy over Mom's possessions. We tried to talk about who should get what, but it just went out of control. We would all be jealous of something a sibling had taken. Dad finally stepped in. He was angry and said, "I'm ashamed of you all. Please return everything you took." Most of us sheepishly returned anything we had taken. Then Dad said, "I will be having an auction sale. If you want it, you buy it. I won't have my family torn apart over Mom's stuff." We tried not to be jealous of the brother who had more money than the rest. But it turned out he wanted very little. Dad also ended up giving each of us a number of Mom's special things before the sale. In Mom's memory, Dad gave the auction money to his grandkids and his church.

* * *

Notes

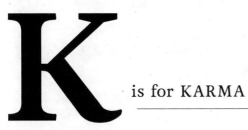

K is for KARMA

Me: (From *Webster's Desk Dictionary of the English Language*-1983) "*in Hinduism and Buddhism: action bringing upon oneself inevitable results, good or bad in this life or in reincarnation*" When we're grieving and believe, or know, the death was caused by someone, we often use the word when hoping for revenge. We want something bad to happen to that person equal to what they made happen to our loved one and us.

* * *

K is for KEEP

Me: What I know is important to keep are the love, memories, photos, and gifts of each other.

But I still have an awful time with my husband's possessions and knowing what to keep and what to find another home for. There are precious things and there is just "stuff." I'm taking my time to make decisions, and other people are helping me. A friend suggested I do a monthly purge. It's important for me to hold on to keepsakes that my grandsons will be happy to have in future years. But I get carried away with what's a keepsake.

Here's where you can give "things" away:

- relatives
- friends

- neighbors
- second-hand stores
- shelters (human and animal)
- agencies that assist the unemployed to write resumes and dress properly for interviews
- churches
- non-profit societies
- recycle places
- garbage
- word of mouth

Here's where you can sell "things." (If you don't want to keep the money, put it in the bank in an education fund for your children or grandchildren, or donate it to a non-profit society):

- garage sales
- consignment stores
- online buy and sell sites (there are many; Google them, but use with caution)
- on your phone
- ads in the paper or on bulletin boards
- word of mouth

* * *

Notes

_____

_____

_____

_____

_____

_____

_____

_____

_____

_____

_____

_____

_____

_____

_____

_____

_____

_____

L is for LAST WORDS

Me: I know without a doubt what our last words to each other were: "Love you lots, be safe, see you soon." "Love you too, I'll be safe, see you soon." Luckily, it was what we always said when one or the other was going somewhere. I just didn't know how far away he was going this time, or for how long. I take some comfort in knowing that the last thing before he left was hearing my voice say, "I love you," feeling my lips on his, and knowing that I wanted him to "Be safe."

Me: My sister died of cancer in a hospice, where we stayed by her side. Not knowing it was her second last night, I talked all night to her, even though she hadn't responded for over twenty-four hours. But I know that hearing is the last sense to go when someone's dying. I talked about the Edmonton Oilers and their incredible team in the early eighties. I named as many Oilers from that era as I could think of, then said, "Oh, hell, what was their little goalie's name? He was incredible but gave terrible interviews." A little voice from the little head on the pillow said, "Grant Fuhr." What!?!? Never give up on what they hear.

Laurie: I can hardly say this, even after eighteen years, but my daughter and I had argued. She wanted to go out with a guy I didn't trust, and she wanted to go to a party where there would be some pretty rough people. I said, "No." After a shouting match, she went to her room and slammed the door, saying, "I hate you!" I thought, *Well, I love you,* but didn't shout it to her as I wished every day I would have. She snuck out her window, as teens have done since defiance was invented. She and two others were killed that night, including the drunk driver—the guy I didn't trust.

Leona: My last words to him in the hospital were: "I brought your passport." He was delirious and hallucinating before he died, and he kept hollering, "Passport. My passport." I went home, got it, came back, and gave it to him. He mumbled,

"My passport," and died within a short time. Did he think he needed it for this final trip?

"Last words are always harder to remember when no one knows that someone's about to die." —John Green

"Tomorrow, I shall no longer be here." —Nostradamus

"Why should I talk to you? I've just been talking to your boss." —Playwright Wilson Mizner to a priest at his deathbed

"You certainly can't say Dallas doesn't love you, Mr. President." "No, you certainly can't." —US President John F. Kennedy responding to Nellie Connally

* * *

L is for LAUGHTER

Me: Laughter is a power. It's a defense mechanism, and it helps heal. Yes, everything's sad, but laughter helps you rise above the moment. People are afraid to laugh, thinking they shouldn't appear to be enjoying themselves around death. That's bullshit. Don't just *decide* you're not going to feel OK, as "it wouldn't be right." It's something your soul has been craving. Laughter has been waiting in the wings to be invited back into your life. Laughter is medicine that we know you won't be taking in double doses right away, but a little bit of it starts to help heal your heart, your mind, and all your organs. It also puts the run on negative feelings like anger and fear.

Me: My husband had a great sense of humor. At his "Celebration of Life" when things got very sad, we got the crowd to sing, "Oh Lord It's Hard to Be Humble," a song he was known for singing wherever, whenever he decided it was too quiet around him. It gave the mourners a chance to breathe again and realize it was OK to laugh, and that was a good way to honor him.

Logan: When Dad retired, he walked miles along the beaches of the Pacific Ocean every day for a number of years. When he died, my brother and I and our families decided that would be a good place to spread his ashes. We all trudged along, focusing on Dad's life, until we came to a relatively secluded spot. Perfect. We all walked into the water, spread some ashes, said some words, and came out. That's when my brother pointed out that we were actually on the edge of the nudist beach! We forgot we were sad and ran off laughing like the fools we were. Thanks for the healing laugh, Dad.

Lex: You won't believe what gave me my first laugh after my sister died. Somebody made a plate of nachos. My other sister asked her son if he had started her car. He said, "Not your car," but it sounded like, "Nacho car." We looked at the plate of nachos and laughed hysterically. Everything became "Nacho…" after that. "Nacho milk." "Nacho business." And finally, "Nacho grief." It became the buzz word when anybody needed a laugh. I still smile when I see a plate of nachos.

Lynsey: After my husband's death, I had a really difficult time with a woman at the bank I used to deal with. She wouldn't listen, had no answers to my questions, and the other employee she brought in to help her was no better. She actually told me I was "hooped." As I was sobbing that I wanted every penny of our money moved to another bank, my sister was rubbing hand lotion on my hands. Later she asked if I knew why she had done that. To calm me? "No, so you wouldn't leave fingerprints on her throat when you choked her." Everything changed from pissed off crying to unstoppable laughter.

Me: I won't get too technical about laughter, except to say it is so important to healing. It cleanses your mind and frees it to enjoy the moment. It cleanses your organs and gives them incentive to work properly again. And it rejuvenates your spirit. You can feel the changes. If you want to know more about how laughter helps you release powerful chemicals and has a powerful physical, emotional, and social impact on you, visit whatsyourgrief.com. Please laugh when you get the chance.

"My body needs laughter as much as it needs tears. Both are cleansers of stress." —Mahogany SilverRain

* * *

L is for LIFTING YOUR SPIRITS

Me: Your grief is yours. And your love and history together is yours. So the choices you make to lift your spirits are yours. You can choose to do this alone or with others. You can choose to come up with ways to rise above the hour or the day. There have been shared arts and crafts days, musicals, albums made, church events, sports challenges, hobbies shared, trips planned, events in nature, or anything that was unique to the deceased. It can be with a few people, or a lot who are close to your heart. I wouldn't recommend a circus of people, though. And ensure you can leave when you've had enough.

Me: It was a "f***ing tree" that killed my husband at the cabin. Friends and our kids waited a few months, and then together we hauled out the big old broken-off tree top that had hit him, sawed it up, and chopped it into smaller pieces. That was the first thing that lifted our spirits. Then we cut down the rest of the tree and did the same thing. We marked it and stacked it to dry. A year later, we invited friends to a wiener roast to celebrate his birthday. After we ate, each person was invited to go alone to the fire, put their piece of wood on it, and send a private quiet message to rise with the smoke to Heaven. It truly took some sadness from our hearts. I put a love letter in the flames. The final lift to our spirits was when everybody sang his crazy song, "Oh Lord, It's Hard to Be Humble."

Me: My daughter lifting my spirits ... again. She, her husband, and our three grandsons bought a miniature tent trailer so Papa Bunny (a little bunny made of his blue jeans and shirts) could still travel with them. They added a tiny hammock, and Mommy made bedding and a small bag to collect souvenirs (rocks and shiny things) for Papa. Then they bought a miniature cabin and put kitchen, bedroom, and deck things in there. Each summer trip and each

Christmas and birthday they find something incredibly cute to add to the cabin and trailer as a gift for Papa. They even found tiny books, a deck of cards, and a teeny tiny wine bottle with glasses. It's so uplifting and brings such warmth as they show you what they added for Papa.

Loreen: When our kids were little, every payday my husband made it a tradition to bring home a coveted Happy Pop for them to share. Later on payday, he splurged on doughnuts for the family. Then it became tradition on special occasions to lay a doughnut instead of flowers on the graves of the grandmas and grandpas in the cemetery, like inviting them to our picnic. It also fed the birds and small animals. So when my husband died, it seemed fitting for all of us to gather around his grave with Happy Pop and doughnuts. We placed a doughnut on the fresh soil so he would know that we would never forget him. It lifted our broken spirits.

Lizzie: Mom's house was the hub of family activity, and her cooking and baking were second to none. When she died, my sister and family bought the family home. They decided that once a month we should get together using Mom's recipes for a potluck meal. We all feel her spirit beside us as we make her recipes. How come they never turn out to taste as good as hers? Mom's photo is set on the cupboard, her spirit is with us, and it's very uplifting to our hearts to share like this with family.

Landon: About once a month, I get out Dad's antique sharpening stone I inherited, and I sharpen knives while I talk to his memory. In the summer, I sharpen the shovels, hoes, and other garden tools that he kept sharp. Same thing. I talk to him while I work. I can almost feel his work-worn hands over mine on the handle of the stone. It really lifts my spirits knowing he's watching me do what he taught me to do.

Leda: It lifts my spirits to wrap myself in the lap quilt my friend made from my husband's blue jeans and shirts. It's like a warm hug from him from Heaven.

Laurie: Every Christmas Eve, it lifts my spirits to go to the country cemetery where my special friend is buried, wait until there's no one around, and blow off fireworks. I choose a schoolhouse for him, and something appropriate for the other nine people I loved and lost. I don't know if it's legal, but it truly lifts my spirits, and there are so many tears in cemeteries that I think everybody there appreciates the excitement and the explosions of color for a change.

Lelani: It lifted my spirits to finish building the playhouse my husband and I had started for the granddaughters. He had all the wood and tools ready, and as I touched what he had touched, I realized his hand was guiding me, and it made me smile instead of cry. When the girls and I had a tea party for Grampa with his favorite cookies, there was joy in that little house.

* * *

L is for LOSING IN EVERY WAY

Lost identity: You have lost your lifestyle, and the planned future is lost. You've lost your identity as mom, dad, sister, brother, lover, husband, wife, daughter, son, grandma, grandpa, friend, confidante, girlfriend, boyfriend, auntie, uncle, cousin, caregiver, provider, or any other role. But we still are ourselves, working to be what we can be.

It's an ongoing challenge as people discover a new loss—besides the obvious— as they move along the grief journey. The list includes, but is not limited to:

- my best friend, my support, my protector, my security, my cheerleader, my sensible side, my source of courage, my rock, my partner in everything, my person coming through the door when it opens;
- my hugger, my kisser, my lover, my toucher, my smiler, my strong man, my soft and beautiful woman, my shoulder to cry on, my source of hope, my dream-sharer, my person to share intimate moments with;
- my story teller, my listener, my news and gossip source, my singer, my person to discuss everything with, my promiser of good things, my joker and teaser, my spiritual partner, my family feud fixer, my shopper, my church partner;
- my bed partner, my pillow and bed warmer, my good night and good morning kisser, my spooner, my toucher of skin to skin at night, my dream and my dreamer;

- my dancer, my entertainer, my bad joke teller, my party planning partner, my wine-drinking partner, my whistler, my game-player, my laughter harmonizer, the daily exerciser, my masseuse, the twinkling eyes across the room, my parenting and grand-parenting partner, my travel companion, my teacher, my child discipliner, my educator;
- my carpenter, my mechanic, my fixer-of-everything, my techie, my rescuer, my planner, my price checker, my tool-and-everything-else organizer, my cook, my cleaner, my banker, my problem solver, my shopper, my list-maker, my recycling and garbage attendant, my alarm clock;
- my ship's captain, my horse rider, my fisherman, my gardener, my sports-of-every-kind partner, my hairdresser, my First Aider, my nail clipper, my barber, my musician, my source of insignificant facts, and lots more.

There are hundreds of other moments when you realize something more is missing. Whether it's something they always did, or said, or how they made you feel, it's gone. It's one more thing to get used to. You will get used to the losses and start to make some gains.

Me: No matter the challenge, I used to say to you: "I have you beside me. I'll figure it out." Now I don't have you in that role, and I say, "What the hell do I do now? How will I figure it out?" But I *will* figure out how to handle those losses one little bit at a time. You are still all those things where I see you in my interior world.

> *"Everything you love is very likely to be lost, but in the end, love will return in a different way."* —Franz Kafka

* * *

Notes

M

is for MEMORIES

Me: If we're fortunate, we have thousands and thousands of good memories, depending on the age of the person who died. And it's those memories that hit hard and knock you off your feet. They make you angry and make you cry a lot. You want the reality you had that goes with those memories.

- Believe it or not, memories will help us every step of the way through our challenges. Hold tightly to them. Treasure them. We need them to survive.
- Memories come at you like waves. Sometimes they're small and gentle thoughts, and sometimes they're tidal waves that knock you down. You will get up, and ironically it may be a memory that pulls you up.
- Photos fill your mind and heart with memories. But none of us want just photos; we want the real person to sit beside us and look at the photos with us.
- Your dreams of your life are shown in those photos, and they were cut short. It's painful to let go of those dreams you had with each other. Let the pain happen and you will be able to look at the photos one day and smile. And then even laugh.
- Videos are great, as they show the person alive, breathing, moving, and talking. But we all want that person to walk out of the video and back into our arms. Right now! Life is not fair. Nobody said it was.
- Then you realize how precious the memories truly are, because we cannot make new memories with the deceased. It's a horrible reality to face, but that's all we have left. He or she remains in these photos and videos in a time and place to be treasured in our minds and hearts. He or she was alive in the photos. And is not now. And that's why we grieve so hard.

"It's true what they say: Love never ends. It's always just as close as a beloved memory, a familiar saying, a quiet prayer." —From a Hallmark card

"Please put this thought from your loved one into your mind and repeat whenever you need to: I have gone, but I will never leave you." —Margaret Thibault

"For those of us still on earth, straining to make something of ourselves, it seems there is no weaning away from the people we love and lose; they are always there, dissolved into the completeness of eternity, waiting patiently—and I suspect, indifferently— for the little resurrection that is memory." —Terry Teachout

"We begin to remember not just that you died, but that you lived and that your life gave us memories too beautiful to forget." —Good Grief

* * *

M is for MESSAGES FROM THE OTHER SIDE

Me: This section will be a godsend to some and bunk to others. But to me and to many, if you see and feel something you think is a message from the other side, it is real to you. Who's to say it isn't? I'm talking about concrete messages you can see, hear or hold. I receive reassurances from my husband that all is well with him and he hasn't left me. He sends a message when I really need one, or sometimes just as a bonus moment. If it makes you feel better to believe in messages, great.

Me: I find dimes everywhere. In places you would never expect them, often at times when I am sad or trying to make a decision or have just accomplished something that he used to do. Blue jays stuck around for the first couple of weeks after he died. They had hardly been in our area before. Then the sad day I had to sign the final papers to close out my husband's business he had worked so hard to build up, there was a blue jay in the tree. It was the middle of January!

From others:

- I saw red cardinals repeatedly after my dad died. And blue jays after my brother-in-law died.
- He loved owls, and I saw owls everywhere, day and night. I hadn't seen them in the daytime for years, but now I did. They were also in strange places: in artwork, crafts, people's homes, photography, books. Everywhere. And a photo showed up of him pointing at an owl in a tree when he was a kid. I found a book I didn't know I had: *I Heard the Owl Call My Name.*
- A streetlight would go off when I drove or walked under it thinking of my boyfriend who had died. This went on for five years. Finally, that summer I fell in love again and became engaged. The first time I said "I love you," a streetlight *came on* right above us. I took it as him cheering for me. I told him I would be OK with this wonderful man, and that was the last incident with streetlights.
- My daughter and her friend had planted daisies in my rose bed. I made them dig them out, but they kept coming back. After my daughter died, I started seeing daisies everywhere. A friend told me that my beautiful daughter was trying to tell me she is now at peace in a beautiful place. I have since learned that the daisy symbolizes innocence and purity, the flower of motherhood.
- A week after he died, I distinctly felt the soft paws of a kitty cat walking up one side of my blanket, across my chest, and down the other side. It still happens, but not as often. He was allergic to cats, but I loved baby kittens. I know he's sending what I would least expect so I know for sure it's a sign. Anything "regular" wouldn't be as noticeable to me.
- We have a sunken playroom for our three little boys. It looks out to the back yard. Our yard is fenced, and we've never had animals come in. About two weeks after my dad died, a big grey cat with beautiful green eyes (his colors) came up to the window, and the boys jumped up on the back of the couch to see it. It stretched its paws up and out, like it was hugging the boys, and it stayed long enough for me to get a picture. I ran outside right away, and it was

gone. Just like that. I knew in my heart it was Papa coming to say goodbye to his beloved grandsons.

- A friend and I went to Peru a year after our four RCMP officers were shot and killed near Mayerthorpe. We were looking for something to help us heal. When we were at the bottom of the HUGE area of Ollentaytambo, four butterflies joined us and stayed with us for at least five minutes. The same thing happened for another five minutes at the bottom of the huge terraces of Maras Moray. Signs? For sure.
- It's been three years and my husband still comes to talk to me regularly in my dreams.
- After my sister died, I had butterflies come sit on my knee quite often when I was outside.
- I found shiny pennies everywhere after my brother died: on the ground, on my dresser, on my deck. Sometimes he'd put them in tricky places, like in my shoe and on the floor of my vehicle. The pennies are worth more than a million dollars to me. They come from him.

Those who find messages say they feel blessed. They pause to think of their loved ones, say thank you, and carry on.

M is for MIRROR

Me: When I first looked in the mirror the day after my husband's death, I saw a stranger. The eyes that stared back at me were somewhat blank, like they were confused by what they saw. There was a strange and new and dark emptiness that I couldn't quite identify. I wondered if that squintiness and those wrinkles on my forehead were what pain looked like. My image was holding a tube of toothpaste and a toothbrush, and I wasn't sure I could feel either one of them.

I said things to that image:

- You coulda, shoulda, woulda. (*But I didn't know what I meant by that.*)
- Get your shit together. (*I didn't know how to put things back together again as I didn't know the process or where I was in it.*)

- Breathe deeply or you'll fall down. (*True.*)
- If I stare hard enough, can I make that person disappear so I can escape from this hell? (*No.*)
- Jesus, my face is like a blank canvas with no color or meaning. (*Yes, for a while, until you start painting your life as it has become.*)
- You stink. It's time to shower and clean up. (*True, sometimes.*)
- I don't know you. (*That's very possible, as I was a stranger to myself.*)
- You can't do this. (*YES, YOU CAN AND YOU WILL!*)

The words changed as the days changed. At one point, all I could say to the mirror was, "You're a widow? What the hell is that? I hate that title. You're supposed to be old before you become a widow."

What I would like YOU to think of saying as YOU stand in front of your mirror at different stages is any or all of the following:

- I am a survivor.
- I am stronger than the storm.
- I will figure out the next step today.
- I will not always be a stranger to myself.
- I will not panic or overwhelm myself.
- I will breathe deeply all day. If that's all I can do, that's enough.
- I will armor up to honor this loss however best I can.
- I will get help when I need it.
- I will make lists of what I need.
- I will accept that explosions can be silent, and I will not hold mine in.
- I will keep myself clean and healthy.
- I will look for things I am grateful for and say "Thank you."
- I will pray for strength and comfort when I need it.

> *"Always remember ... you are braver than you believe, stronger than you think, more beautiful than you imagine, and loved more than you know."* —Christopher Robin to Winnie the Pooh

* * *

M is for MONKEY MIND

Me: You can call it what you want, but to me, "monkey mind" is when your brain goes into overdrive, and you cannot shut it off.

- It jumps from this thought to that thought, like a monkey from tree to tree, forgets what it started thinking about, and is distracted like the dog in the movie *Up* (Squirrel!).
- It wants answers, but you have forgotten the questions, or you remember the questions, but you can't find the answers in the muddle inside your brain.
- Your monkey mind goes back to many things before the death and then worries about many things in the future. Your fears and your anxiety go into overdrive, thanks to monkey mind.
- You're trying to focus on the person in front of you speaking to you, but your mind is jumping all over the place and picking up a word or two, so you don't really know what was just said to you.
- Your mind wonders what the funeral director or banker or lawyer or whoever said you should do. But monkey mind was too busy to let you concentrate for a moment.
- You're trying to multi-task and you can't even focus long enough to single-task.

We can't seem to shut our thoughts off. To me, that's a brief description of monkey mind. And I'm pretty sure from what I've heard, most of us go through it in our grief. That's why we have a pen and paper, or we have a good friend who has a pen and paper and makes a suggestion we sit down and take some deep breaths. In through the nose and out through the mouth. It also helps to light a candle and focus only on the flame for a few minutes while breathing deeply.

* * *

M is for MOUNTAIN OF GRIEF

Me: Weeks or months after a death, you awaken to a strange mountain in front of you with rugged peaks, solid walls, and sheer drop-offs. You've felt its presence for several weeks, but you actually see it in your mind today. You're lying in a spirit-drowning swamp of grief, and you start to realize it's too dark to stay there. You take a deep breath, you stand, and you look towards the mountain. Soon after, you take a tentative step.

Different people want different things as they take hold of their grief and slowly set off on this difficult climb. The list of what we want to do includes, but is not limited to:

- Leave the **chaos** behind and find some order, some calm, some peace.
- Leave behind the **"monkey mind"** and find some kind of organized thoughts and actions.
- Leave the **insecurity** behind and find confidence again.
- Get rid of the **fear** and find the courage to carry on.
- Get rid of the **denial** and find acceptance
- Trade the **imbalance**, the feeling of being off-center physically and mentally, for a sense of balance.
- Leave behind the **panic** and find self-control.
- Get rid of the **misery** and find self-worth and happiness.
- Leave the **confusion,** the brain fog behind and find order and clarity.
- Stop being **incoherent** and become coherent.

Some said they wanted to stop feeling **ignorant** because they don't know how to handle this new and horrible situation. But they are not ignorant. There are no instructions or road maps. Everyone can and will become more knowledgeable through experience and learning.

The climb isn't easy, and there won't always be progress, but the view and life on the other side of the mountain is worth the work. Nobody can set a time limit or a route for the climber. Or tell them what shoes to wear and when to start. It takes a big, bigger, humongous effort to let go of misery and re-discover happiness. Even if at first it's just a little flower they bend to pick. Or the wind in the trees. Or a child's laugh or hug. Or a sunrise or sunset.

We are all capable of surviving great ugly whacks of pain, and the power to do it is sitting quietly in our overwhelmed brain. Take a deep breath and bring your power to life. The mountain's waiting.

"There's no way to shorten the journey of grief," —unknown

"If your path is difficult, it is because your purpose is bigger than you thought." —unknown

"You never know how strong you are until being strong is the only choice you have." —Bob Marley

"Grief never ends... but it changes. It's a passage, not a place to stay." —unknown

* * *

Notes

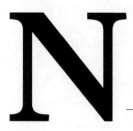# N is for NIGHTMARE

Most people now know where Humboldt and Tisdale, Saskatchewan are. But none of us can wrap our minds around the unfathomable nature of the horror the good people from there and many other places are suffering. Their hearts pump nothing but pain while trying to grasp the reality that sixteen people were killed and thirteen were seriously injured in an earth-shattering bus crash involving a young hockey team on April 7, 2018.

The Broncos were pumped physically and mentally for the hockey game they were headed for. Instead, half of the team was taken to the morgue, and the other half was rushed to hospital by ground and air.

The first responders—the RCMP, the ambulance crew, the fire department, the STAR's crew, and innocent witnesses—walked into that nightmare, and God only knows what they saw, heard, touched, and smelled. And it was a sure thing that the hundreds of people involved had nightmares afterwards. And some will still have nightmares.

We may not have known anybody involved and have never seen any horror of this magnitude, but we can relate to hockey players. We can relate to young athletes. We can relate to sons and daughters, sisters and brothers, grandchildren. We can relate to teenagers getting on a bus to go from Point A to Point B. We can relate to small communities. We can relate to first responders. We can relate to love. And we can relate to death.

So we grieve for all affected by what happened this day, something that is so deep it doesn't really have a name. Event? Tragedy? Horrible crash? None of these even touch the magnitude of the losses. We sit on the periphery and our hearts ache for every person involved, and nightmares sneak up on us too. But there's a difference. In this case, we awake from our nightmare. Those involved don't.

Nancy: I had such terrible nightmares after I found my son dead that I was terrified to fall asleep. So I stayed awake, or partly awake, for weeks. At first I thought it was a mannequin, but I knew it wasn't. I didn't remember anything for a while after, except seeing a mannequin. When I fell asleep after a couple of days, it all came back to me in a nightmare. And that same nightmare recurred for months. After the first horrifying two weeks, I finally had to go to a doctor and a psychologist. It's been three years, and it's still there, but I have a little more control over it, and the nightmares are almost non-existent.

Norbert: I'm speaking not only as a retired police officer, but also for ambulance workers, medical staff, and firefighters. So many people use the word "nightmare" for a bad day at work, or a mother-in-law who's a bitch, or their bad holiday. They have no idea that when you see and hear so many horrible deaths that happen so many times, and you're called to them, THAT becomes a nightmare. And the nights that follow are FULL of nightmares you just can't handle, physically or mentally. So you pace or jog, and smoke and drink coffee and watch TV to avoid it. And you talk to your partners. But you don't sleep, because of the nightmares. And one day you are diagnosed with Post Traumatic Stress Disorder, and a psychologist explains it all to you. And there are meds and mind exercises that help. And my dog is a Godsend. But I have to admit, I'm still always waiting for that nightmare to slip out from the closet or from under the bed if I go to sleep.

Nelles: I found my brother hanging in the granary. Even after six years, it takes very little to set off the nightmares. Sometimes they just are there.

* * *

N is for NOTIFICATION OF NEXT OF KIN

Me: I have been with many RCMP officers over the years as support when they do a Notification of Next of Kin (NOK). I assure you that next to seeing a young person or baby dead, or people's body parts strewn across the highway, the worst thing an officer has to face is going to the family to do an NOK.

They change lives forever once the words are out of their mouths. They know they will face terrible horror, fear, denial, or anger on the faces in front of them. First the officer will ask about the relationship to the deceased to be sure they are with the right people. Then they have to be clear and concise: "I'm so sorry. I have some very bad news. (Name) has died." They have to say the word "died" or "was killed" so it is clearly understood why they are there.

They will witness screaming, total silent shock, punching, arguing, fainting, running away, puking, or other loss of bodily functions, painful crying, or a slammed door from someone trying to keep the bad news out. There are as many reactions as there are NOKs. And none of them are right or wrong. They just are. And the officers return to their detachment to deal with the tragedy and the family's response the best they can for their own survival.

While most of the NOKs are very sad and awful, there are those that the police learned a lesson from:

Nellie: I went with the RCMP at 3:00 a.m. to do an NOK at the home of a widow well into her eighties. The young officer shared the sad news that her sixty-something-year-old son had died of a heart attack at his home. She paused, looked at the officer and me, nodded, said, "Tenk you for telling me."

She then said, with her pleasant Ukrainian accent, "Now you come eat. Eat. You're too skinny. Come eat. You shouldn't be out at dis time of night." She hadn't taken "No thank you," for an answer. This sweet little woman was bustling around her kitchen, fixing traditional Ukrainian food. I asked, "Is there someone we should be helping you call? Do you have any other family?"

"I have a dotter," she said. "She lives in Calgary. But she'll be asleep."

"Well, I could help you call her if you want."

The little woman looked at me like I was not too sharp and said, "We'll call her in the morning. He's dead. He's not going anywhere." With that, sugar was scooped into three coffee cups, and it was accepted that this strong woman was handling her grief in her way: cooking and looking after others for now. Bless her heart.

Nick: It was a notification of Next of Kin, and this one was a bit different. The dad had died, and the grown son was called to the house. As we waited for body removal, the son showed up bearing a shovel. I prayed he wasn't going to dig a grave and try to quickly bury dad on his farm. Nope. Mom told me he didn't get along with dad, and neither did she, as he was a "cranky old bastard nobody enjoyed being around." The son was sure he had buried money in tobacco tins along the fence-line in the back forty. The facts of the death and info were shared with Mom, whose parting words were: "Yeah, thanks. I gotta get out there and be with my son." Sometimes family love carries quite a price.

* * *

N is for NORTHERN LIGHTS

Me: One of nature's most incredible light displays brings me comfort and a reminder there's a much more powerful force than we humans. It's the dancing of the Northern Lights, or Aurora Borealis. They're a spectacular array of luminously brilliant colors ranging from streams to rippling curtains, to shooting rays that give the night sky an extraordinary eerie glow. Sometimes you can even hear the Lights crack like a whip when they weave around like a snake. They show us mere mortals their power and beauty.

Nia: My husband and I believed that a child conceived under the Northern Lights would lead a gifted life. We now believe that's true and not true. Our "Northern Lights" son died saving his girlfriend's life. He was a hero, but he still died. Maybe gifted has a wide range of meanings.

Nathan, seven years old: The Northern Lights are all the dead people in the sky dancing for the live people on earth. People who die get a sparkly color when they go to Heaven, and that's why they're Northern Lights. And they all dance to angel's music. Mommy says Papa and Gramma and Grampa dance there.

Noreen: I was in a home when a baby died of Sudden Infant Death Syndrome (SIDS). Mom was with the police and I was in another room with children aged four and five. They were talking about where pets and people went after they died. The five-year-old then asked, "What did Baby do bad? Gramma said if you did something bad, the Northern Lights would come down and kill you. She said the Northern Lights got our cat because it dug up people's flower beds And the Northern Lights came and killed our bird because it pooped all over everything."

Maybe Gramma thought it would be okay to lie about where the bird and cat went, but it wasn't. Can we *please* stop threatening children with scary bullshit about death? There's enough for them to sort out and try not to be afraid of in life. Let's make the most of what beauty we're blessed with, like children and the *beautiful* Northern Lights.

* * *

Notes

O is for OFF BALANCE

Me: Somebody kept pulling a rug out from under me. I kept stumbling, like I was doing poorly on an exercise balance board. I was mentally and physically off balance, and I couldn't find the center of my being or my stance. I found that being dizzy from not eating or sleeping properly doesn't help your balance. I just needed to slow down, breathe deeply, accept that it was normal to be off-kilter, and try to improve each day.

Olivia: I used to watch my son in his saucer-based stationary walker trying to move towards a toy. He lunged and hollered and waved his arms and kicked his feet, but he just wobbled unsteadily and went off balance repeatedly. He didn't move forward. He knew what he wanted, but he was stuck and off balance. Even after two months of grieving, I can still identify with that. But I'm getting better.

Orville: I got so frustrated when I was trying to do chores and I kept stumbling and leaning too far one way or the other. I had done the same chores thousands of times and never found myself acting like a tree in the wind. I was awful god-dang mad at myself, especially when I realized I couldn't focus in my head either. Sure glad my cattle knew what I was supposed to do, as I wasn't doin' too good. My daughter explained to me after that I was doing OK. I was just in the first hard parts of grieving.

Odette: At first, I found it physically strange to walk, as I felt like I was missing a step or walking on wooden legs and tilting one way or the other. Then what really threw my mind off balance was dealing with my bank and not understanding the changes to our accounts. I wasn't prepared for that. Neither was I prepared for the will to be so outdated. Now, THAT really made me wobbly and threw my whole life off balance. It seemed the more I tried to accomplish paperwork, the more mixed up I got. And a true fact took me off balance: each signature on paperwork made him less and less likely to be alive. I knew that. I just felt I was being banged on the head with it. It took almost two years and the help of an accountant to get my finances worked out, which is a dizzying experience. I now feel more balanced emotionally, physically, mentally, and somewhat socially.

Ona: It seemed whenever I bent forward to put on my shoes or pick something up, my toes couldn't hold me, even when I gripped the floor. I felt like I was going to fall on my forehead and kind of lunged for balance. And whenever I tried to think of the best way to move, it would seem like too much this way, or too little. That went on for months.

Onastasia: I kept envisioning half my brain missing, putting my whole life off balance inside and out. My husband took it with him when he died. I had to slowly grow another half a brain, and it seemed to take a long time before it gave me balance back.

* * *

O is for OTHER DEATHS

Me: There doesn't have to be a death of a person to grieve. It can be the loss of a dream or other plans. It's important to grieve miscarriage, divorce, children leaving home, being fired, retiring, and anything that leaves you with a sense of loss and emptiness. You have every right to grieve as you spend time figuring out the meaning and unfairness of it and what it means to your life.

Me: There are other deaths that turn into complicated grief that often needs intervention from medical grief professionals. The circumstances may require referral from the situation. Some of these might be murder, death of a child, police or front-line worker deaths, a family member who has found a suicided loved one, kidnapping deaths, prenatal deaths or mother or child or both, multiple deaths, a person who has caused an accidental death, an extremely gory death, and deaths where the body has not been found. I have been and would willingly be with any of you as part of your process, but only if you're also meeting with a professional mental health provider.

* * *

Notes

P

is for PAIN

Me: It's been two years since the love of my life died, and I felt the pain might do me in at first. I remember somebody saying, *"Hell came to the door and moved right in."* With the help of many, I now realize that same pain does not last to that degree forever. When you're broken and pain rules your every moment, life has a way of bringing you people who are the healers you need. They help stitch up the broken heart and ease the pain. They can't take your pain for theirs, but they endlessly listen to whatever you need to say about your pain, they hold you when you cry, and they hold your hand when you take tentative steps. They help you walk through the pain.

Paulette: The pain was so hard to describe, but it was almost like I was dying too. As if someone ripped me open without an anesthetic and kept poking all my organs in there with knives. I didn't know if the blood in my veins was like lava burning me or like icicles stabbing me. It felt like both. I can't really describe it because it was beyond words. I believe grief hurts so deeply because we loved so deeply.

Petra: When my daughter was killed, I was told later that I didn't speak at first. But I thought I begged for someone to take the pain away with a gun. The pain wouldn't stop, and apparently I screamed until I was taken to the hospital and given a strong sedative. I was told later that through the next few days, I asked them to stop sticking pins in me everywhere. Not only in my heart, but my chest and stomach and everywhere. When they convinced me that there weren't pins in me, and that I could count on a great little pill, I didn't want reality. But eventually it hit me. Hard. As part of becoming mentally healthy enough to go home, I had been slowly weaned off my strong saving-grace pills onto a lighter anti-depression pill. One month's worth at a time. I wasn't happy at first, but I realized I could feel again, and, thank God, my family was waiting for me. Now after three years I can think of my beautiful daughter without my mind checking out. It's all become a huge permanent scab I try not to pick at.

Peter: My doctor asked me if I needed anything for the pain. I said no, because I was afraid I would either eat the whole bottle at once, or I would be a drooling druggie for the rest of my life. I thought of alcohol or street drugs but was afraid of the same thing. I needed a pill that would turn time around so this wouldn't be happening. I needed this unbelievable pain removed from my broken mind and body. I wanted there to be surgery for it. I thought briefly of killing myself, but I knew I couldn't do it. And I was afraid of all the ways I thought of dying. I realized somewhere in my fog that I didn't want my life to go away. I just wanted this excruciating pain to go away so I could breathe and not feel like eels were eating my insides. Eventually, my body crashed, and I started sleeping better, which helped. And eventually, with help, the pain diminished.

Pat: Looking back over the four years since he died, I hang on to something a good friend told me: *It won't always hurt this bad.* And she was right. But at the time, as the shock is wearing off, it hurts worse than you can ever imagine. You're no longer numb. You're ripped apart, and boxer's punches land everywhere inside and out. But eventually the pain is no longer excruciating. It's now bearable. And it does get better. I just don't think it ever goes away completely. Maybe …

"Death is not unique, but your pain and grief are." —unknown

"I really thought I was slowly dying from mental and physical pain, unhappiness, loneliness, and despair. But later I realized I was slowly living through it all." —unknown

"When life puts you through a tumbler, it's your choice whether you come out polished or crushed." —Elisabeth Kubler-Ross

"We learn that we are irrevocably changed by grief."

* * *

P is for PATTERN OF GRIEF

Different experts say there are anywhere from three to nine or more stages of grief. Pick out the ones you can identify with as you go along: shock, denial, anger, bargaining, acknowledgement of reality, depression, testing and looking for meaning, and acceptance. They are all normal and acceptable places to hang out, so don't panic when you find yourself in one, skipping one or more, or experiencing two or more at the same time. It's just a general guideline, not a list of boxes to check off.

Me: There was no cut and dried pattern to my grief except shock. When I found my husband dead, my mind shut down in shock. For about twelve to sixteen hours, I made no sense to anyone. I felt no emotion because I wasn't connected to my mind.

Denial seemed to take over for those same hours. I kept asking who died, where, who found him, and how many died. I couldn't make myself believe my husband was dead, even though I had found him. When our family and friends came to the house, I accepted the *idea* that he was dead, but the reality was harder to grasp, because I remembered nothing. Your head may accept it, but your heart certainly doesn't.

I skipped the anger and bargaining and went to depression. There were waves knocking me over. I didn't want to go to bed, and then I didn't want to get out of bed. I could find nobody to blame, so I didn't really feel anger except towards myself for not knowing what to do now. It's relatively common for people to get angry at the one who died, but for whatever reason, I didn't. To me, bargaining was futile, but ... was there some way I could talk to him just once more?

Depression came and went, and I started testing and looking for meaning. I had gone back to work fairly soon after, as it was my safe space with my safe people. Finally, I went for groceries and other necessities. I met with a limited number of friends. I tested my ability to be with others and to be in public. Sometimes my attempts worked OK, and sometimes they didn't work at all, and I scurried home.

It's been two years, and I have gone through minor depressions a couple times. I may eventually reach total acceptance, but I feel that's a very big final step. Everything about my life has changed, and I'm finding ways to deal with the fact my husband is no longer a major and loving partner with me. But I think it's OK that I don't accept it totally at all times.

Everybody grieves differently and experiences different stages for different lengths of time. Grief is so personal. Don't let anybody tell you exactly what you should experience and for how long. Everything you feel is valid. But if you feel really stuck in one stage, or extremely overwhelmed for any length of time, get professional help.

* * *

P is for PERSPECTIVE and PERCEPTION

Me: Our personality's way of looking at things, the words we hear, the pictures in our minds, our previous experiences, all the situations we have been in and are in, determine what our mind sees and how we will react. Your *perception* is your recognition of the situation, your immediate thought and impression and how it makes you think. *Perspective* is seeing a broad view of events and deciding their nature and relationship to you. Like a painting has *perspective:* some things are bigger than others, and some things are further away than others. Both these things determine much of what you think you see and how you react.

Paul: I'm an artist. I know perspective is important. But for about the first year, nothing was in perspective, the size or distance it should be, and every day it changed. It's like those trick pictures. What do you see, the beautiful lady or the old hag? It seemed I looked at things differently, and different things were critical and bigger than life for that hour or that day. It's almost impossible to keep perspective when it comes to early grief. But thank God it doesn't stay that way.

Paula: I tried to keep things in perspective, but so many things got blown out of proportion in my mind and heart. A word, an act, a thought—all became bigger than me many times and changed my perception of my struggle. That's when I would really melt down. After a while, the death of babies and young children helped me put it in perspective that at least my husband had been given seventy-nine years to live a good life and leave great memories. Not that I would ever advise comparing losses, but sometimes it helps to look at the big picture of the world of life and death.

Penny: My perception of death used to be what I saw from a distance, not somebody close to me. My perception was death was part of life, people eventually got used to a different life, funerals helped the family and friends, and it was very sad. That *was* my impression. After my husband died, my perception changed. I see now that death rips your heart out, it turns you into a stranger, it takes a village to put you back together, and yes, you will get used to a different life ... eventually. But you go through a pile of painful shit before you can put things in perspective.

Peggy: My first experience with death was when my gran died when I was ten. I was told she went to Heaven, and my perception of death was Gran's beautiful spirit going to a beautiful place with clouds and harps, and God smiling at everybody because He was happy they came home. I'd love to have kept just that perception for everybody. But now that I have experienced the pain of other deaths that were totally out of the planned cycle of life, my perspective has changed. My beautiful perception now has some dark scribbles marring it.

* * *

Notes

_____

_____

_____

_____

_____

_____

_____

_____

_____

_____

_____

_____

_____

_____

_____

_____

_____

Q
is for QUESTIONS THAT PROBABLY WILL NEVER HAVE A SATISFACTORY ANSWER

Me: There are several questions around every death that can never be answered adequately.

- *Why?* Is the big one. *Why him? Why her? Why now? Why that way?*
- *What were his last thoughts? Did he suffer?*
- *Why were they there? Where were they going on that unfamiliar road?*
- *Would she have known she was dead?*
- *Did he know it was happening?*
- *Was she scared?*
- *Could I have changed the outcome? Or prevented the death(s)?*
- *Does she see me from Heaven?*

Many of the questions are about what was going on inside the person's head at the time, and not even police, medical specialists or pathologists can answer that. But the big question that goes through everyone's mind is "WHY?" And once we can accept that there probably isn't an adequate answer to that (other than realizing life isn't fair, and Mother Nature's sometimes a bitch), we can work on sorting out other information.

Quentin: Just so you know, I'm under a doctor's care, and my head doctor thought it might help me to put this out there. My wife was killed in a car crash, and I was in my vehicle fifteen minutes behind her. *Why? Why in a crash? Did she see it coming? What did she think at the last second? Why was that other vehicle on that stretch of road? Did she call for me? Could I have changed the outcome if I was there sooner? Will that picture always be in my mind?* In my wishful moments, I see myself saving her. If I couldn't have saved her, at least I could have died with her. I know the questions I ask will never be answered, but they still stick in my mind. As my life is happening without my wife, I know a fact: I will miss her every moment and forever feel guilty about saying we needed to take two vehicles. No question.

* * *

Q is for QUILT

Queenie: When my friend arrived at my house, she found me sitting under a pile of our fourteen-year-old daughter's clothes, running my hands through the remnants of the past, feeling the fabrics against my soaking wet cheeks, inhaling the essence of what had been, trying to capture the spirit of our daughter through the last things that had touched her soft skin. We had buried her five months before, but I still needed to see and feel her clothes. I couldn't get rid of them.

My friend took the clothing and a month later handed me a quilt with beautiful squares and triangles of the golds and reds and oranges and greens and blues of our daughter's clothes. There was a memory stitched into each square. And there was a pillow, with the stuffed sleeves of our daughter's favorite baggy sweatshirt dangling from each side, ready for a hug. I just can't thank my friend enough, and I can't tell you how comforted I am by feeling our daughter sending us hugs from Heaven.

Me: I knew an older couple who lived a tough but loving life together. Their love and respect for each other garnered attention in the community.

Then sadly he died. She often spoke of his gentleness, his love, and the many years she supported his love of pony chariot racing, while he supported her love of sewing. She decided she had held on to his shirts and jeans long enough, and it was time to do something with her grief. She lugged her sewing machine into a crafting weekend with friends and brought her husband's warmth from the past. Carefully she sewed a frame out of pieces cut from his blue jeans. The squares were photos of his pony chariot days transferred onto fabric. In every photo, his face showed his love of life and racing. She filled the corners with triangles cut from his favorite shirts.

Lost in love and memories, she finished the front of the quilt that weekend. The fabric artwork was designed for the queen-sized bed she had shared with him. There is so much love in a memory quilt.

Me: My friend made a quilt each for our son and our daughter out of their dad's well-worn blue jeans and shirts. I am so grateful for this kindness. Our daughter's quilt patch in the middle reads, "Past the Sky and Around the Corner" which was the way they described their love for each other. And our son's reads, "Hey, Buckshot!" a forever reminder of their relationship. There are even a few patches from my dad's dress shirt from the 1960s. Then, because she is such a special friend, she took part of my dad's shirt and the front of my husband's shirt, with the pocket still there for Kleenex, and she made a pillow for snuggling and to catch laughter and tears. Now we still feel him near us, and we all give and get special hugs day and night.

Me: Another friend who has a quilting business gave me a "grieving quilt." It's bright, colorful, soft, and beautiful, and without fail, it perks up my mood when I put it over me. Someone made one for her when her husband died, and she found it such a beautiful and useful gift that she shared the idea with me. I am so grateful. It's been two years, and the need and importance of the quilt still touches my heart and makes me smile.

* * *

Notes

 **R** is for RAGE, REVENGE, and HATE

Me: Rage is an extreme feeling, and revenge is the action you want to take. Hate is also a deep feeling, but it can actually be less dangerous than the other two. While anger is natural and mostly controllable, rage and revenge are dangerous if left untreated. Your family won't be able to handle your revenge. They have enough to deal with right now without you ending up in jail.

Rage, revenge, and hate are such strong and heavy feelings and actions. Left untreated, they leave you giving away valuable energy in a negative direction. Grief energy gets depleted just from trying to breathe. Try to step back from, or postpone, revenge by turning towards your family's needs. Definitely seek professional help if you can't control it.

Ray: I experienced rage for a long time when a drunk driver killed my child. I couldn't eat. I couldn't sleep. I couldn't have a decent conversation with anybody. I could only seethe and think of ways to get even. I needed revenge. I was exhausted. My mind was shutting the world out, shutting down to anything except revenge. My blood pressure was at stroke level. My muscles were always tight and painful. My organs weren't working properly. It lasted until I got sick enough to end up in hospital. I'm still angry, but my psychologist and medication have helped me control the rage that was controlling my life.

Rachel: I had been deeply and darkly angry after a coward murdered my daughter. I somehow kept my rage in check until the court case, when I became out of control. I was a stranger to myself. Day and night I thought of how I could shoot him in the courthouse. How I could throw acid on his face to wipe that smirk off. Drinking a lot only fueled my rage. One day I looked in the mirror and knew if I killed him, I'd be no better than him. Although I did seem to lose my mind for a while, I kind of got it back when he went to jail. I also talked to a psychiatrist. But when he ever gets out, I don't know how I'll react. And of course, I know that wouldn't help my daughter or my family. I've got my psychiatrist's office number on speed dial.

Rita: For a long time, people avoided me. I boiled with rage. My body posture was loud and clear. My eyes and my face were vocal even when my mouth wasn't. My mouth only spoke ugly sentences that I thought were truths. Thank God a friend took me to a psychiatrist for help, "just to meet her." A great psychiatrist met me head-on and gave me a safe place to let the rage out. Plus, the pretty little pills helped.

Rick: All that consumed me for over a year was how to get even with the drunk driver who took my daughter's life. I conjured visions of really bloody and painful revenge. And one day I realized I was descending into an incredibly dark abyss that I might not get out of. With help from mental health professionals, I stopped giving him the energy and mind control that I needed so I could grieve my daughter properly. But I still want to live long enough to see him dead and buried.

> *About healthcare workers: "At least they understand that when I'm fucking angry let me be fucking angry, and sometimes the dark humor I use is the only thing to get me through the pain." —Shirley*

> *"Bitterness causes corrosion and breaks down whatever it touches, wherever it settles." —unknown*

* * *

R is for REACTIONS and RESPONSES TO GRIEF

Me: You may wonder if your reactions or responses at this time are "normal." You may feel like you're out of control, or even insane. NO. *You* are normal; it's the *situation* that's abnormal. ***I stress, everything is grief-normal except to react***

with suicide or homicide. It's difficult to define what's going on in grief, but here's a partial list from when I was Victims' Services coordinator. They're divided into **Feelings, Thoughts, Physical Reactions, and Behaviors** you may experience. Any of the four areas may overlap. Everyone is different, so the package of "you" may include, *but not be limited to*:

Feelings (what may be going on in your chest or stomach area):

Anger or Rage	Emancipation/Relief	Loneliness
Anguish	Emptiness/Loss	Numbness
Annoyance	of purpose	Overwhelmed
Anxiety	Fear	Sadness
Bitterness	Frustration	Shock
Depression	Guilt or Self-Reproach	Vulnerability
Disorganization	Hate	Yearning
Edginess, Nervousness,	Heartbreak	
Irritability	Helplessness	

Thoughts (what may be going on in the mind):

Blame	Inability to follow	Regret
Concern for others	a conversation	Sense of presence
Confusion	Indecisiveness	Worry about everything,
Dazed	Jealousy	including finances
Denial	Lack of concentration	and paperwork
Desire for Justice	Lack of confidence	Preoccupation with the
Disbelief	Lack of focus	deceased, or with death
Disorganized thoughts	Memory loss	around you, especially
Disorientation	Mental fog	those close to you
	No sense of time	

Physical Reactions (what your body is experiencing or telling you):

Breathlessness	Headaches	Changes in appetite
Digestive upsets	Heart palpitations	Lack of energy
Dryness	Hollowness	Loss of equilibrium
Extreme Fatigue	Hurting all over	Nausea

Off balance mentally
and physically
Oversensitivity to the
5 senses

Psychosomatic issues
Sense of unreality
Sexual disturbances
Shock

Shakiness
Tightness and tenseness
Weakness everywhere

Behaviors (what you do as a result of your feelings, thoughts, and physical reactions):

Absentminded actions
Avoid reminders
Blame any and all
Become obsessed with
true crimes through
books, TV police
dramas, social media,
local court cases
Become obsessed
with who you believe
caused or contributed to
the death
Become obsessed with
or withdraw completely
from religion and/
or spirituality

Break, burn, or tear up
important things without
waiting to see if you will
need them in the future
Chain smoke or
begin smoking
Dream or
have nightmares
Eat everything
or nothing
Drive recklessly to prove
you're invincible, or
decide you will never
drive again if it was a
car crash

Hoard your loved
one's items
Increase alcohol intake
Look to the wrong place
for help
Lose all
emotional control
Move or make big
changes too soon (a year
is recommended)
Refuse help of any kind
Release anger
inappropriately
Sleep a lot or not at all
Withdraw socially
(become a hermit)

There are other things people have mentioned that have helped them:

Accept help from friends
and family
Seek encouragement in
many forms
Discuss Gratitude
Hold on to hope
Give and accept love all
around you

Accept religious /
spiritual support
Make lists alone or with
a friend and feel relief
for the small things that
get done
Remind yourself to be
thankful for the many

good things and the
many memories you had
Talk to somebody you
trust, a mental health
professional, or a
grief counselor

Remember: you are not alone in your reactions and responses, and you are not losing your mind.

Our reactions and struggle with grief are what makes us human, and in grief it hurts and is confusing to be human.

During initial reactions: I know I seem like an invalid, but I need to make some choices. Even if they're as simple as do I want to stand up or lay down. Coffee or tea or water? Answer the phone or let it go to machine? Answer the door or lock myself in? Talk to you or not? It returns some power to me, and I really need that just now.

My grandmother once gave me a tip: In difficult times, you move forward in small steps. Do what you have to do, but little by little. Don't think about the future or what may happen tomorrow. Wash the dishes. Remove the dust. Write a letter. Make a soup. You see: you are advancing step by step. Take a step and stop. Rest a little. Praise yourself. Take another step. Rest a little. Praise yourself. Take another step. Then another. You won't notice, but your steps will grow more and more. And the time will come when you can think about the future without crying. —Elena MIKHALKOVA

* * *

R is for RELATIONSHIPS

Me: *Every* person grieves differently. When a loved one dies, there's a huge shift in relationships of the living. Either relationships become deeper, or they don't survive. In-laws become closer to the family or they become distant. Husbands and wives hold each other close or can't stand to look at each other. Family members are torn with their own grief. The reasons for this are your own, but it's very important each person be allowed to grieve in his or her own way. And respect becomes a two -street.

Ridley: I was glad my husband went back to work when our son died, because we couldn't be there for each other. We grieved so differently. We could hardly look at each other, because we would see the grief and the haunted eyes but not be able to talk about it. We were told that it's important to be allowed to grieve in our own way and to respect each other's needs. After a few years and a marriage counselor, we eventually came around to what we have now.

Rebecca: I hated my husband when our son died. I had said "No" to the party and he had said "Sure." He didn't make the crash happen, but I had to blame someone. He blamed himself too. He was beating himself up and couldn't let his feelings out. He grieved quietly, and I grieved loudly. I shrieked and cried and drooled and talked to myself. We separated for almost a year, and each went to a grief counselor separately, then a marriage counselor together. We're still not totally together, but we're working towards the deep love we had when we created our son.

Randall: Nope. We couldn't make it and it was probably for the best. She gave up on life completely. She wouldn't let me or anybody else help her or be near her. I tried so hard to understand. He was my baby too. And I know grief is forever, but after two years of her shutting me out completely, I realized I couldn't do this. I'm still working on my own grief, with help. And I think she's glad I left.

Randie: My mother-in-law blamed me and shut me out completely. She didn't want me helping or making suggestions on anything for the funeral. We had no children, so it was easy for her to have nothing to do with me. I had to fight for rights and I'm glad I did. I have to say she may have given birth to this wonderful man, but now I hate her as much as I loved him.

Ruthie: Our daughter-in-law turned into a nasty out-law. When she and my son were married, she smiled at me, but now I know it was a fake smile to please him. We saw them only a few times a year, so I didn't realize how much of a buffer our son was until he died and she turned on me in an instant. I couldn't hug her, I could have nothing of his, and I could make no suggestions about anything. At first, I tried to get along, because I felt our son would want the wife he loved to remain part of the family. Her response was, "Don't bother."

Reba: When my sister died, my mother died with her. She was still here, but it took years for her to remember she had a living daughter who needed her attention and love more than ever. I was fourteen and I grieved my sister, but sometimes I was jealous of how much attention she got in death. I got attention by becoming a wild teen to punish my mother. It was way worse for both of us. I understand it now that I'm older, but it was really hard at the time. We get along much better now. My mother is actually an amazing person. Maybe I was selfish, but that's what I remember most.

* * *

R is for RELIEF

Me: There is a real relief after certain deaths, but so often people won't say it out loud. Maybe because we think relief is synonymous with joy. Relief actually means ease, or comfort. There are lives that carried an oppressive heaviness that actually eroded the lives around them. They needed to move to the next world for mental and physical reasons, but death came slowly. And finally there was relief.

Rita: After several years of threatening to kill himself, my friend's husband did just that. My friend had confided in me that she felt such relief it was no longer her burden to carry. But she said she felt so guilty at feeling relief. It's OK and it's human nature to feel relief. She had tried to get him help several times, but it was to no avail. The secret was well kept. Now with his death, she would never have to worry every day about where, when, why, and how. She said she will be OK living with her relief, and her mental health worker is helping her deal with her unnecessary guilt.

Ria: My grandmother and my grandfather died within a week of each other. They were elderly, but both very active people. They loved each other dearly.

They both were terminally ill with cancer. She took treatment; he chose not to because he didn't want to live long without her. She went through all the challenges of chemo and radiation. He went through her challenges with her. They both became gravely ill. They begged to die together, and I believe they brought it on quicker than expected—a week apart. We all felt such relief that they were together and out of pain. But that didn't lessen the terrible grief we felt.

Ronnie: I hate to use the word relief. It sounds so uncaring. But my wife had had so many different illnesses and complications in her last years that I couldn't help but wonder how long she could do this. When she finally died, I privately breathed a sigh of relief that she was finally at peace. I felt guilty and kept my relief a secret in case people didn't understand it. So imagine what a weight was lifted off my shoulders when my children approached me cautiously with their relief that their mom wasn't suffering anymore. Thank God we could share our relief with our grief.

Reg: My brother was an addict—alcohol, drugs, you name it—and for the last fourteen years lived on the streets. I often lost contact with him, but somewhere along the line there would be brief information about him. So when I got word that he was dead, I felt relief. Relief for him, no longer on the streets, and relief for me and my family because we didn't have to worry about him anymore. And yes, if you're not using my name, relief from the shame of having one of our family living so horribly on the streets.

Rex: My father had tried to kill my mother, but she lived and he went to jail. When he was released, the son of a bitch went after her again, only this time she again lived and he died. That was the biggest relief of her life and mine. She had been terrified of him. And no, there was no guilt about how we welcomed his death. Only sweet relief.

* * *

R is for RESILIENCE

Me: Resilience may seem foreign in the first few days of our grief. We feel we will never snap back, never get through this, never get rid of the pain. But you are resilient. You got up this morning. You breathed. You got dressed and walked. You spoke a full sentence. You are reading this. That's a good start. You'll notice there are positive distractions around you, and they will help you adapt. That is resilience. Hope plays a big role. What do we hope or need for the immediate future? What choices do we make, and what trust do we put in ourselves to get there? Do we stay mired in our misery, or do we try to step outside of it when we can?

Me: Resilience is answering the question: How can I reconstruct my new life one little movement at a time? What will anchor me in the present so I can focus better?

- maybe it's a person you love;
- maybe it's you in the mirror;
- maybe it's a small plan for the day, a small but definite decision;
- maybe it's a stone held solidly in your palm for grounding you at this moment;
- maybe it's a task you set yourself physically, mentally, spiritually, or emotionally;
- maybe it's a bit of new information;
- maybe it's a day or half-day back at work;
- and the list goes on …

You can't connect to your old life, and it's tough to connect to your new life. What is your new life? What will it be like? That's up to you. Believe it or not, your resilience will help you to eventually regain your new life balance: physical, mental, emotional, social, work, spiritual.

Rhoda: I held a tiny babe in my arms and experienced a feeling of beauty. In this wee bairn's face was a promise of hope, and healing, and innocence and a future that will go on no matter how I handle my grief. To understand that is a sign of resilience. We all have our own way of finding our resilience. I was told it depends on our history, our experiences in life, our loves, and our personalities. What it comes down to in reality is: it depends on us. We are the masters of our own resilience.

Roseanne: "Exercise" may be what some people turn to to feel more resilient mentally and physically. But for those of us who feel overwhelmed by the word, I call it "movement." I walked up and down stairs when I thought of it. I got up from my chair and walked around the house at first and then around the block. When I was sitting and my legs were just dangling there, I would raise one foot at a time and trace the alphabet in the air. But most of all, I would remind myself all day to breathe deeply. All that made me feel I was becoming resilient. I was doing what I could to improve my health so I could move on.

> *"Resilience is our ability to meet with difficult feelings, and not only trust our capacity to adapt and recover from them, but to find something redemptive hidden within adversity. It takes a lot of energy to distance ourselves from pain, not only do we become more vital by entering into relationships with our feelings, but that resilience grows into a place of refuge for others." —Toko-pa Turner, excerpts from* Belonging.

* * *

Notes

S is for SHOCK

Me: Shock is what happens in the first few minutes after learning about a death. Shock is a state of mind. There is a numbness that our brain shoots through our body so we don't have to take in this horrible news all at once. Shock may last a few minutes or a few hours.

Sometimes, as in my case, your brain actually takes flight to protect you. I found my husband dead after he had been hit by a tree. Apparently, I was able to do the right things: phone the police and tell them everything. I covered my husband with a blanket because he was cold.

When I was in Victim Services, I told people that it's common to hold it together initially in shock but fall apart when help arrives and the professionals take over. That must be what I did. I completely lost my mind and hardly knew my name. I was told that for over twelve hours, I seemed to re-set my mind every ten minutes or so and ask the same questions in the same order. Questions I used to ask when I was called out by the RCMP in Victim Services. I wouldn't know because I remember NOTHING from those hours that night. Not even arriving and finding him dead. The first thing I remember was arriving home the next morning. In a way I wish I could remember, but in another way, I know my mind has shut it all out to protect me. I often wonder if my husband took the bad stuff from my mind when his spirit left him. I don't apologize for my reaction.

Sarah: I was in shock for a couple days, even though I went through the motions. My mind was numb while we planned the funeral. I was numb while I walked and talked and sat and spoke and cried. But I always felt cold, and I shook a lot. I remember very little of that first week. The more paperwork I signed afterwards, the more unlikely it was that he was alive. I knew he was dead, but I didn't have to accept it all in one time period. I actually wanted to stay in shock longer.

Stan: I tried to punch the police officer immediately, as I didn't want to hear those words come out of his mouth. He was wrong. He said my daughter's name and then said, "dead." Those don't go together, and he had no right to come into our house and say that. Then he said, "impaired driving," and I knew it couldn't be her. My wife let out a scream, and I looked at her like she was a stranger, even as she fainted. I just stood there. Somehow the police and Victims' Services got supportive people around us, and I don't remember the horrible details except for small pieces over the next few days. I was told we had both gone into shock. Once in a while, I still feel that shock sneak up on me.

Sheila: My thoughts struggled to understand the people talking in front of me. My brain stopped working and my body started to shake. Everything went weak, and there seemed to be a piercing battle in my head, but I didn't know what was happening. Victims' Services gave me warm tea and put me to bed with a warm blanket for a couple hours. They stayed until my family showed up.

* * *

S is for SPECIAL DAYS

Me: It doesn't matter when Death Day happens, that date is seared into your mind. In the past 365 days, you celebrated special days. Now for the next 365 days, each special day will be a first without your loved one. First Christmas, first Easter, first Father's Day, Mother's Day, Thanksgiving … and so on. There's no doubt they're tough, and it depends on how close to Death Day they happen. The absence is loud and obvious, so it's not advisable to treat it like "the elephant in the room." It can't be ignored, but it helps to be prepared:

- Choose beforehand what you want to see or do. An empty chair at the table lets you feel you are including him or her.
- Do you want a sit-down meal or a buffet? Which one would feel better?
- Choose beforehand who you will ask to do the things the missing person did. Don't let it be a sad surprise when there's nobody to slice the turkey or make whipped potatoes.

- Light a candle. Or several candles. Children especially like to light a candle of remembrance.
- Include that person in the grace.
- For Thanksgiving, we always hold hands and go around the table to say what we are thankful for. Include him or her in your thanks.
- Plan a craft or activity for after the meal for adults and children.
- Accept there will be tears, but there will be good feelings also.
- When people start arriving, ask them if they will put a very special memory of the deceased down on paper. Or they can put just a word about that person. The messages can be read or displayed on the table after the meal. There might be tears, but there will also be laughter as everybody reminisces about the relationship they had and the special things about it.
- A woman told me her husband hated shopping, so for her birthday, Valentine's Day, or Christmas, she always bought something she wanted, wrapped it, and pretended to be surprised when her husband gave it to her. It made them both happy. She has continued to do that.
- Buy a Christmas ornament for him or her to add to your tree. Frame his or her photo and put it as the angel on the top of the tree.
- Call and talk to friends.
- Make a donation to a non-profit in your loved one's name and make it a tradition.
- Take a trip.
- Scale down the celebration, but still have it.
- Write your feelings down, or paint them, or use another medium.
- Have a potluck using all the favorite recipes he or she left behind.
- Keep busy. If you can't keep busy at home, volunteer at a non-profit center, a shelter, a soup kitchen, a food bank, or anywhere that needs you.
- Deliver gifts secretly to someone in need.
- Remind yourself, it's only one day. You can do it!

* * *

S is for SUICIDE

Me: My husband met SJ at a riding stable full of rescued horses in Arizona. SJ was a Vietnam vet who had severe flashbacks and suffered from what is now recognized as PTSD. He took my husband and his friend out for a horseback ride in the Arizona desert. He had flashbacks, a gun, and they shared several cold beer along the way. Hmmm. A few months later, SJ shot his horse, burned his saddle, and it's believed he completed suicide in the desert. My husband and his friend felt guilty and often wondered if they could have helped him. But they also realized that as good a guy as he was, his brain was completely out of sync with life because of the horrors of what he saw and experienced in Vietnam. They felt there was a special place in Heaven for the SJs of this world. They also realized how important it is for society to rescue veterans as well as horses. Isn't that the truth!

Me: I was phoned by a mother who was told by her minister that her son would burn in hell because he had taken his own life. Really? Stop and think about that. Have you spoken to the devil to ask what the criteria is? Is there not a loving God in your world? Wouldn't a loving God welcome the person who dies by suicide as gently as the person who dies any other way? Maybe the brain of the person holding the gun or pills or whatever told them they were living in hell on earth. Rev. Frightener, you are not judge and jury, and it's not your decision who goes up and who goes down, and you had no right to control your flock with fear. People who complete suicide are in deep pain, physically or mentally or both. I fully believe that in death they are swaddled and receive extra strong arms around them as a welcome to help them heal before they move higher.

Sally: I learned that many people who attempt suicide do not want to die. They just need the mental or physical pain to go away. Unfortunately, our son died in that process. At first in our anger and pain, we asked, "What could he have been thinking? Why would he bring such pain to us?" While a select few may have intended to bring pain to certain individuals around them, we now know our son didn't. He had been injured in a farm accident and was in a wheelchair for life. We finally found his note, and he had convinced himself he was doing us a favor because he was a burden. He was sooooo wrong.

Sybil: My sister told me that when her baby died and her husband divorced her and she lost her job, it felt like she had sunk into a deep, dark hole with slippery sides that she couldn't climb out of. She felt we would all be better off if she died there. She said when she was luckily put in care to recuperate, she got the help she needed. There she met a woman who said her brain was chemically unbalanced and her doctors were keeping her in there to "get her motor running smoothly again." She had gone off her meds and slid quickly into a deep suicidal depression, so she was back again. Suicide is not necessarily selfish, nor is it an act made with a rational mind. We can't enter into the person's brain, so of course it's too easy to judge from where we sit.

Steven: It's hard to forgive myself for not seeing the signs before my dad completed suicide. I know everybody says there are no visible signs, and that they're only "signs" after the fact. We're not meant to see them or know what's going on. I know we can't be in that other person's mind, but I wanted to be. The saddest thing about suicide is that the person sees his or her life with no hope. And love is not enough.

Facts about suicide:

- You're not always meant to know it is going to happen. It's often a secret that is living in only one person's mind.
- There may be some warning, but you probably won't realize the significance of those words and actions until after the death.
- Once a person makes the decision to complete a suicide, he or she usually appears to be at peace and doing better mentally. The pressure is now gone. But you couldn't have known that.
- It is "completed" suicide, not "committed" suicide. Committed suggests a sin, and who are we to determine suicide is a sin?
- Completing suicide is not usually brought on by just one thing. It's much more complex. It's like being on a deadly river. It's flowing calmly on top, with the occasional rapids, but churning furiously underneath, ready to suck you down and into the falls. It's not just the falls; it's all the negative tributaries, hidden whirlpools, and rapids before the falls that lead to the final act.
- The vast majority of suicidal people don't want to die. They just want a way to make the pain go away.

141

- Suicide grief is different from other grief. Not more, not less, just different, because you believe it could have been prevented or stopped.
- Anger felt toward the deceased after a suicide is sometimes deeper, more powerful, and longer lasting than you expect.
- Suicide has no boundaries: economic, social, age, religion, racial or ethnic groups. (Google "Facts about Suicide" for the breakdown of this information if it will help you with your grieving.)

Me: There are many articles on suicide prevention, intervention, and postvention on Google. Plus, your medical community has information. If you need it to help with your grief, please ask for it.

* * *

S is for SUN

Me: There is *one* thing you can count on right now. And that is the sun rising and the sun setting.

- No matter what has happened, and what you choose to do about it, the sun will still rise, and the sun will still set. Every single day.
- Within your twenty-four hours, there may be chaos. But the earth does its orderly spin, and the sun makes its orderly appearance to bring day, and its disappearance to bring night. You may not notice beauty right now, but once you're ready to look for it, you will find it at sunrise and sunset.
- No matter how dark it gets, the sun is going to rise again. And as long as you keep breathing in between those twenty-four hours, you've done the best you can, and the sun will reward you.
- If you had what you consider a bad day, the sun will still rise the next morning, and you can see what the new day brings.
- Those who died yesterday had plans for this morning when the sun rose, and those who died this morning had plans for tonight. Don't take life for granted.

Wake up—kick ass—repeat.

"*When it looked like the sun wasn't gonna shine any more, God put a rainbow in the clouds.*" —*Maya Angelou*

* * *

S is for SURVIVOR GUILT

Me: Survivor guilt is extremely difficult to come to terms with. Why did you survive when others didn't? You feel you deserved to die right alongside your friend or family member. You can wear the cloak of guilt as long as you choose to, or you can take a real in-depth look at the situation with a professional and figure out how to shed that heavy burden. It can be done.

Spencer: I was the "other brother," the one who survived the crash when my brother and his friend were killed. I keep seeing him laughing, with his arm over the driver's seat, showing me photos of the girl he had set up as my blind date. Why couldn't I wait to see her? Now he's dead because I distracted him and said, "Quick, quick! Show me her photo." You have no idea what it's like to live this way. I had a broken arm, and people said they were relieved I was hardly hurt. They didn't know for how long I wanted to be hurt really bad and die. I have a broken heart and a guilty blackness in me. In spite of my mom's best efforts, I don't know if the guilt will ever go away. But every once in a while, there's a little bit of hope, and an uncle who helps me talk about it. The RCMP were really good too.

Serena: I didn't think I had that much to drink, but I was wrong. And I was wrong to get behind the wheel. And I was wrong to turn to my friend to laugh about a guy hitting on her earlier at the party. I didn't see the moose until it was too late. Too late to take that split second back. Too late to bring my friend's life back. All I seem to be able to do is stare at nothing and say, "It's my fault she's dead. I was drinking. I should have died too." Dad and my lawyer are not happy with me for saying that, but I want to be punished. I survived. Lots of people around me are helping me. But others hate me, as they should. But maybe my purpose now is to talk to people in prison. And maybe talk to kids in schools about survivor guilt. I'm an expert.

Scott: My friend was the athlete, the smart guy, the one who had his life planned. I'm nothing except the survivor of the drinking contest. All I can believe right now is I should have been the one to die. It would have been easier for a lot of people. I cheated on how much I was drinking. But I cheered him on, because I'm the guilty jerk of the crowd. My mom and dad said maybe I should go to different schools to talk about drinking too much when you don't know your limits. Maybe. Maybe I'll tell them not to be an arsehole friend, because the grief and the fact you survived rip your guts out.

Sonny : For a long time I felt like I was the guilty person for being the sole survivor of the crash in which my brother and his friend, who was driving, died. I suffered broken bones and a broken spirit. My parents were broken zombies. The guilt drove me to become the perfect son to make up for what I felt I had taken from them. He was everything to them. I was just the kid brother. I wished over and over that I would have died instead of him. I was told later I suffered from survivor guilt. I didn't really care what you called it. Trying to be perfect didn't do much good, and the pain was too much, so I tried to drown it by drinking and doing drugs. My parents had no idea how I hated hearing, "And this is our other son" when they introduced me. That was like a knife in the heart. They had no idea how guilty I felt that it was him who had died and not me. Finally, a teacher I liked took me to the school psychologist and I spilled my guts. The guilt was so strong I couldn't stop crying. I still cry, but I'm coming to believe I don't need to carry the guilt that was ripping me apart. And I realize my parents also felt terrible guilt, because their grief swallowed them up and they didn't see what was happening to me.

Suki: I was the only survivor of a small plane crash. Why? What about my friends? Why did they die and I didn't? I looked at their families and friends at all three funerals, and I think they wondered the same thing. I think they were angry at me for surviving, even though they were kind to me. I know I didn't want them to have to see me alive while their loved ones were dead. I went into hiding until my sister made me go see a psychologist friend of hers. I'm better, but I still don't understand why I lived.

* * *

Notes

T
is for TATTOOS

Me: In 2019, my husband was to have turned seventy in July, and our daughter was turning forty in May. We were planning a big party. Suddenly, there was no party. There was my husband's funeral in April. Our daughter now had a different birthday request—for the two of us to get a tattoo to honor Dad. Tattoos are the greatest permanent things for preserving memories. Mine is on the inside of my left forearm where I can see it and touch it whenever I need to. It is in his handwriting, using his pet name for me—a beautiful line from a letter he wrote to me, and his signature. There's also four Xs for his family, and three Os, which were changed to hearts, for the three little grandsons he absolutely adored. A colorful infinity symbol borders the tattoo.

Our daughter got a dandelion going to seed with her dad's writing to her on the stem, and eight little symbols—a bird, a star, a cross, a fish, a dragonfly, a butterfly, a feather, a flower—among the floating seeds to represent the nine people she loved and lost in her life. There are beautiful colors added in the background.

Tattoo artists are such generous people. There's no limit to what you can ask for. I looked through their books, then Googled tattoos, and came up with hundreds of sites and literally thousands of suggestions. Wings, hearts, the person's face, the person's writing, infinity symbols, messages, feathers, flowers, butterflies, dragonflies, vehicles big and small, pets' faces and paw prints, hobby representations, crosses, ribbons, angels, halos, dates of birth and death, a line from a song or poem, and names in all scripts, are just some of the suggestions. These can be in any combination, color, or font, giving you thousands of choices. And they can be put anywhere on your body where you have skin. Some of the messages that stood out to me were:

- Your wings were ready, but my heart was not.
- Daddy, I was never ready for you to leave.

- You'll be with me wherever I go.
- I am because you were.
- You were my most precious hello and my hardest goodbye.
- You left me beautiful memories, your love is still my guide, and though we cannot see you, you're always at my side.
- The good memories are for the tough times.
- Your death shattered my world completely. Nothing looks right and nothing feels right.
- Our memories make me stronger.
- "Someday" smacked me in the face too soon.
- 'Til death do us part, we said at the start. Now it's here, it breaks my heart.
- I was not built to break, but I'm shattered without you.
- Can you feel the pieces of my heart that went with you?

Tricia: When my husband died, I got a tattoo with what we always said to each other: "You will forever be my always." Dates and angel wings are added. This is all on the outside of my left forearm so I can see it whenever I glance down. It's like we're still saying it to one another.

Tanner: Our precious baby daughter was just a few hours old when she died. We knew she would always live with us and our two-year-old, who had been waiting for us to come home with her. So my wife and I got tattoos we could see every day. It's a branch of a tree with mama bird and papa bird perched on it, close to little bird. Baby bird is flying away towards Heaven, but always in our sight. At first the tattoo reminded us how broken our hearts were, but now there's a sense of peace in looking at it and knowing she's near and will always be our loved baby in Heaven.

* * *

T is for TEARS

Me: I didn't cry much at first, as I couldn't believe he was dead. I was in total shock. Then I was busy with others ensuring his Celebration of Life would be as he wanted. I cried some when people hugged me. And in the middle of the night. But as soon as the Celebration was over, reality hit. I cried until I couldn't breathe. I cried until I threw up. I cried in roaring anguish that hurt my throat. I cried into a towel as a Kleenex couldn't hold all the tears. And now, two years later, the tears still leak out uninvited and drip down my cheeks and wet my pillow. But I will never apologize for the flooding that continues. Death hurts. Forever.

Theresa: I thought I could show people how strong I was because I didn't cry very much when my husband died. I held it in. I breathed it back. And inside my body, it grew and grew. One day I looked at his photo, and I exploded and had a meltdown. Thank God for my psychiatrist. She helped me realize how "strong" attitudes hinder healing. Now I know who my friends are, as they accept my tears.

Tom: When my son died, I thought if I worked hard enough in my eighteen-hour days, the pain would go away. The day I fell apart and let the tears take over my life, I accepted I was stupid. Grief was bigger than me, and tears are OK. They were a way of finally releasing my pain and starting to work through it.

Me: There's a microscopic photo series by Rose-Lynn Fisher that shows the difference between tears of grief, joy, laughter, and irritation. It was put on Facebook by "I f* * *ing love science," and says: "Tears aren't just water. They're made up of water, salts, antibodies, and lysozymes, but the composition depends on the type of tear. There are three main types—basal tears, reflex tears and weeping tears." Fisher evaporated the tears and studied what was left. They all appear as a close-up aerial photo.

- **Tears of grief** are spread out different linear lengths, horizontal and vertical, with uneven empty spaces between them, like an abandoned warehouse district in the Town of Tears, Population 1. It seems the tears are trying to rearrange themselves around this big empty hole in the center.
- **Tears of change** look like a thick, closely-clustered shrub area with a small airport building plunked into it. It's not quite sure what it's doing there.
- **Laughter tears** are what you'd expect—rippling and splashing in all directions, different sizes, different shapes, like water movement caught below a very thin sheet of ice, trying to break out.

- **Onion tears, or irritation tears,** are like the impressions left by beautiful ferns pressed into frost on your window.

"Tears are God's gift to us. Our holy water. They heal us as they flow." —Rita Schiano, Sweet Bitter Love

"Sometimes crying is the only way your eyes speak when your mouth can't explain how broken your heart is." —Varsha Sharma

"There is a sacredness in tears. They are not the mark of weakness, but of power. They speak more eloquently than 10,000 tongues. They are the messengers of overwhelming grief, of deep contrition, and of unspeakable love." —Washington Irving

"You know that a good, long session of weeping can often make you feel better, even if your circumstances have not changed one bit." —Lemony Snicket, The Bad Beginning

"The sorrow which has no vent in tears may make other organs weep." —Henry Maudsley

"The most painful tears are not the ones that fall from your eyes and cover your face, but the ones that fall from your heart and cover your soul." —women working

A strong woman is not the one who doesn't cry. A strong woman is the one who cries and sheds tears for a moment, loves beyond all faults, fights battles nobody knows about, then gets up and fights again. - unknown

* * *

T is for TERMINAL ILLNESS

Me: There are terminal illnesses that are slow to take over the body and those that work faster. But you always know the end will come sooner than you want. Every terminal illness is cruel. Cruel to the ones dying, and cruel to every person around them who loves them. And also cruel to the medical community around them who don't have a magic cure. You're not prepared, no matter how much time they and you are given.

TeriLee: My mother died slowly. Cancer is cruel in that way. It eats and eats a human, and even when it should be full and fall off like a blood sucker, it continues. When it gets tired of eating at the breast, it goes to the next meal, and the next, and the next. That's what I kept imagining as my mother fought for her next breath. I realized I had been grieving her before we got to this point. Her last two days were a struggle. Her skin was draped over her sharp joints like a sheer curtain. Mom's hair looked like a newborn baby chick resting on the pillow, teeny tiny tufts of sparse feathers randomly visible. And that beautiful, soft, toffee-brown face I had loved so much from the moment I was born was now sallow, gray and sunken. No dimples, no sparkle, no joy, no eyes open watching me like the protector she is. But damn it, she tried her best to smile. The only time I heard my mother use the F word was near the end, when she said, "I will continue to fight this fucking cancer in the most ferocious way I can find. If something happens to me, I want my children and grandchildren to know I did not go quietly into the night." And she did not. She was strong. She took each battering with dignity. She still made jokes until this last week. But now, because I love her so fiercely, I have to accept she could not fight forever with the cancers she had. There is so much more to tell about Mom, but mostly that my beautiful mother did not go quietly into the night, but right up to her last breath fought that fucking cancer. Within my grief I have such admiration and appreciation for her.

Therese: My husband had eight bouts of cancer in five years. Every one was in a different place. And until the last one, the brain cancer, he never gave up. He never lost hope. He was determined he would see his grandson graduate from school. Thomas was in Grade 12 when Grandpa died. When he did graduate, he said, "I'm making sure Grandpa's with me today, Mom." And he tucked a photo into his shirt pocket under his grad gown. We receive beauty as a gift in unexpected places in our grieving.

Timothy: I don't understand. With all the money raised for research, and all the medicines available today, why, why, why can't we do more for cancer patients? The people at the cancer institute are incredible. They do everything in their power to help heal and make it easier for the patient and her family. We loved them. But the quick changes in my wife in six months from before cancer until she died were heart-breaking. I believe there are cures—I just don't know where.

Tucker: After my wife died, I heard rumors from friends that there is a cure for cancer, but the big drug companies and pharmacists make too much money on cancer drugs to admit it. My friends read rag-mags and specialize in conspiracy theories, which provides a sense of fake powerful knowledge. I know there are millions of people with hundreds or maybe thousands of different types of cancer, and what works for one will not work for another. And trillions of different combinations have to be tested. What I'm frustrated with as just your average Joe Blow is that a lot of money seems to go for advertising and administrators and CEOs, but what is the real percentage that goes into research, development, and testing? Maybe we all need to look for facts. No matter what, my wife is still dead.

Terry: My father had ALS, Amyotrophic Lateral Sclerosis, named after Lou Gehrig, a famous baseball player. Dad was my best friend, my sports hero. I was scared when he became clumsy and lost control of his muscles. And I was terrified when they diagnosed ALS and said there is no cure. Over the next five years, he became somebody who couldn't move, couldn't speak or swallow, couldn't do anything with me. But I realized he hated it even more than I did. I knew he could still hear and see, so I sat with him, talked to him about important things in the outside world, and we watched all kinds of sports on TV. I told him I love him. But oh, how I hated the disease that was dehumanizing this wonderful athlete, father, and husband. He was still my hero 'til the end. It's been almost three years since he died, but I still struggle with the unfairness of it all.

Trinity: My healthy husband's personality started to change, and he started to display anger and became somewhat violent. After an episode, we went to the doctor and discovered he had an inoperable brain tumor. He was put on meds that helped somewhat, but it quickly got worse, and I found myself not liking this stranger he had become. It was very confusing and challenging, as I still loved him but didn't like him. And I *hated* his tumor. It was so unfair. When he died, I was angry at myself for not being more understanding. I held out hope and denied everything for part of the time. I was still confused about how fast things changed and how ugly the whole situation was. I so deeply love and miss my husband, but the terminal illness challenged everything about our life.

Toni: My mother made her secret plans as soon as she heard she was terminal with only months to live. For her seventy-fifth birthday a couple weeks later, she called a family party, with twenty-three of us there. No gifts allowed, just donations to non-profits. She made all our favorite foods with her special recipes, played upbeat music, and we laughed, danced, and thoroughly enjoyed each other's company. She wanted lots of photos taken. As we left, she handed us a wrapped box and said, "This gift will help you remember everything special about this day. Don't open it 'til you get home." Each gift was a keepsake of hers that each one of us had loved for a different reason. It was a shock that there was also a photo of her, and her eulogy she had written, below which she had added: "DO NOT phone me or visit me for two full days. Give yourself time to digest this with your siblings, and then alone. I have accepted the diagnosis with gratitude for the life I lived. Daddy is waiting for me. Please respect my wishes." The letter enclosed was also a shock, but beautiful and full of love. It helped us make her last days ones of laughter, not all sadness. The overpowering sadness and grief for all of us came the day we said goodbye to this incredible woman. She knew she had raised a family who loved and trusted each other and would look after each other in grief.

Tristan: My proud father thought he could fix or beat anything, so he was very angry when he found he was terminal and couldn't beat his illness. When he had to go into care, he made us promise not to watch him go downhill "to an ugly carcass." After a certain point, he forbade us to visit him. The nurses would let us know when he died. He wanted to be alone, and he wanted us to remember only the powerful him. He reminded us he would meet up with Mom when he died, so he wouldn't be alone. His demands were even harder than his death.

Terminal illness does not define who you are. It's what's happening to you. People have trouble differentiating, so you have to let them know you are still you. - unknown

* * *

T is for TIME

Me: Depending on what you're doing or feeling, the hands of a clock either spin around or don't move. It doesn't register and could be day or night, one o'clock or ten. On the clock, the minute is disconnected from the hour, the hour is disconnected from the day, the day from the week, and the week from the month. You may look at a calendar and ask: What week is it? What day is it? Should I be better by now? Should I be in another "stage"? There is no set time for grieving. You must take it in your own way, doing what you can in that moment, or in that day. No one can tell you when to "move on." Time alone doesn't heal. It takes time and *intention*.

Me: Sometimes you might wonder about the day that just went by. Was it a skinny day that had long tall hours in it? A scrunched-up day that went by in spurts? A stretched-out day that went on forever? Or an "I forget" day? All are OK.

Trish: It's been six months, and I still can't talk about his, y'know, passing, without losing it. I hate it when people ask about it and ask how I am, and I have no answers for anything. But they make me feel like I should be getting better. The only one who makes me feel OK is my good friend who says, "Take your own time."

Tiffany: I noticed people didn't say "death." I wasn't able to either at first. It was a whole freakin' five months before I could speak clearly and openly about it. My daughter had finally broached the subject. I thought I was shielding her from pain by not talking about it. I was very wrong. But with help, I got smarter. She could talk about it and needed to grieve differently from me. Her time frame was different from mine in her own days and ways. And damn it, don't let anybody tell you how long anything should take for you or your child. You work on doing what's right for both of you. If you want assistance on how to handle your child's grief, ask a professional.

TerriAnne: We grieved totally differently after the death of our son. I had to lie in his bed, cover myself in his blankets, hold his clothes, and spread his photos all over the house so I could see his handsome face at all times. I lived like that for at least six months. My husband didn't want photos out. He wanted our son's room closed and to leave his clothes in the closet or give them away. Luckily, my husband worked out of town most of the time for the first six months, so I could do it all the way I needed to, in the time I needed. He wanted to work through his pain in his own time. He hoped that if he worked hard enough, he wouldn't think of it every minute, and that time would magically take the pain away. Perhaps having time apart at the first was what saved our marriage, as I think it's something like 75 percent of marriages fail after the death of a child. The loss and the differences in grieving take over the whole relationship. I have to say with a LOT of time, and new ways of communication, the edges of the shards of glass in our hearts did smooth out. And with hard work and intent, our marriage survived.

Thomas: I was told once you've been married a long time, it doesn't take as long to "move on" when the other half of you dies. That's so wrong. Whoever said that has never lost a major piece of their heart. "Time will heal all." "Give it time and you'll move on." Well, excuse me, but bullshit. It's six months since she died, and time has not taken the pain away. Lessened it some, but it's still pretty sharp. The only good thing about time is that we had forty-nine years to make more good memories than most couples. And the children and their spouses and all their babies help me find some joy in the time I spend with them.

Talia: I lost all concept of time and days. I couldn't tell you if it was four minutes or four hours before the police arrived. I couldn't tell you if it was 10:00 a.m. or 3:00 p.m. when my sister arrived, or on a Thursday or Saturday. Was it three days between the death and the funeral, or seven? You say it's time to do this or that? Why? What does that mean? I have to look at a calendar to see how long he's been dead. Since I'm struggling so much with time now, don't try to tell me how long it should take for me to stop crying, or to get out of the house, or to sort all his belongings. Shut up. Time stopped when he died. It will continue to go on without me for a while.

* * *

T is for TRIGGERS

Me: Everyone left behind has had their mind tricked momentarily by an action, a sound, a sight, a taste, a smell, or a touch. Anything that used to be "his" or "hers" that triggers a memory, no matter how simple it seems. My friend's melt-down came when she couldn't find "a pair of fucking pliers." Tears were triggered when I couldn't find ant killer; when I sold his tractor after six months; seeing his blue jeans hanging on the clothes rack; eating grapes with salt on them; pulling a cipaille out of the oven, memories ad infinitum. Little triggers that were bigger than me at that moment and brought tears. Your triggers will be yours alone.

Me: *I want to make it clear that there are more intense and terrifying triggers in complicated grief that can cause uncontrollable panic attacks, psychotic breaks, and mental breakdowns that require immediate medical care. I will not presume to have the words to address them here.*

Tessa: That morning I thought maybe I felt strong enough to walk downtown and get the mail. I had been driving everywhere so I could run in to whatever business, do only what was critical, and run back home to the safety of home and my quilt. Today I walked. For a second I felt good, but then my chest got tight as I saw someone getting into their vehicle, their back turned. For just a second, I saw my husband—the grey hair, the broad shoulders in a red and black plaid work jacket. My husband's jacket. My husband's hair. His broad shoulders. But not him. The blood rushed to my face, my ears rang, and the tears came again as I ran home. I would try again tomorrow. And I would drive.

Tanya: I was sitting in his big recliner chair, and I heard the click of the back door. I spun around, delighted for a second, as I thought he'd come home. It was probably only a millisecond of hope, but then in anger I shouted out loud, "He's not coming through that door again. It's a fact." That sound triggered reality. I buried my face in his pillow and cried until I was sick.

Todd: I still smell her hair stuff, and it makes me cry. I take a bite of a certain food she liked, and I choke on it. Seeing a dad hug a daughter makes me cry. A silly song we sang when she was a toddler makes me cry. An invitation to her friend's wedding sent me over the edge. She should have been the bridesmaid. I just can't get away from triggers. And maybe I don't want to, as the memories are precious.

Actions: Looking for something of his or hers you can't find or don't actually know how to use: in the garage, the kitchen, the garden, the office ... anywhere and everywhere. Things only he or she was familiar with can trigger tears. Many more actions that you take accidentally or on purpose can trigger memories.

Sound: Certain footsteps on a floor, a cough, a laugh, a sigh, a voice, a horse whinnying, a door opening or closing, a tractor or vehicle, an ATV, a song, a bad joke. And much more.

Sight: A flash of certain clothing, a certain build or walk, a baby being lifted, a skier, a fisherman, handwriting, a half-finished project, a tree, the cabin, a horse, tools, kitchen items, a hand reaching out, a certain cup, dancing, sports, PVR'd programs, same color vehicle going around the corner. And much more.

Taste: Grapes with salt on them, cold milk, a certain beer or any other alcohol, smoke, a campfire hot dog, favorite food, peanut butter, whipped potatoes, ice cream with chili, berries, strong coffee or tea. And much more.

Smell: The scent of a pillow, baking, hospital, perfume or after-shave, newly-mowed lawns, fresh cut hay, anything in nature, the garage, a cigar or cigarette, frying onions in butter, popcorn, even farts. Coffee in the morning. And much more.

Touch: The feel of blue jeans, pajamas, a pillow, a tool, a quilt, a saddle, certain clothing, a favorite pet, the corral, grass, couch, animals, his chair, freshly washed sheets. And much more.

There are literally thousands more triggers that give us a split second of hope and then bring on the tears. They will surprise you, slam you, catch you off guard, and even make you question your sanity. Triggers are your brain adjusting to the new reality. They won't always and forever bring tears. Some of them will eventually just bring you a good memory.

* * *

Notes

U

is for UNIQUE CELEBRATIONS
OF LIFE

Me: There are literally thousands of ways to honor the person whose life you are celebrating, from standard funeral practices and words to unique celebrations. I hope this brings a smile as I share a few that I've experienced or been told about:

- His garage gig band played his favorite songs at his celebration, not well, but with enthusiasm.
- His niece brought her high school paintings that he loved and decorated the hall.
- Some friends wrote poetry to tell stories about him and then read some poetry he had written, which was very bad and funny.
- I lit fireworks in a rural cemetery after the loss of a beloved young man, because there is so much sadness around graves. I chose fireworks that celebrated the personality of the people I knew and missed greatly. I blew up the schoolhouse for my precious young friend. I got twelve balls of light for the price of ten for my Scottish dad, and a basket of silver and gold flowers that looked like a geyser for Mom. And so on. I don't know if it's legal, but it felt good.
- At my uncle's funeral, each of his many grandchildren had drawn and written a word about him on helium-filled balloons, and each grandchild told the guests which word they chose. Then enough balloons were tied to a cowboy boot to make it levitate about an inch off the stage! We could almost hear him laughing over that.
- We used his cowboy boots for vases for a wildflower bouquet made by a friend he really respected.
- Everybody was given a beer and a noisemaker as they came in the door of the machine shed where we held the meal. Then at 3:00 p.m., we cracked open

the beer to toast him and used the noisemakers, which he loved. No stupid hats, though. Just cowboy hats.

- For our trucker friend, we had ten big trucks that followed the hearse to the cemetery. When they asked if anybody had anything more to say, we all blew our air horns twice. Then his widow climbed in his truck and blew the air horn once, making it a twenty-one-gun salute. The snow actually fell off all the trees surrounding us, which was fitting because he loved nature.

- We got half a dozen of his best friends together the day after the funeral and we all went to a friend's cabin at the lake. We did exactly what we did the last time we were all together with him. We had a swimming race to the island. We had a canoe race. We took his pontoon boat out and dove off it as many times as we could without taking a break to see who lasted longest. Then in the evening we had a contest to see who could light a fire the fastest without matches, and we roasted hotdogs. There was lots of laughter, but God, there was a big hole in our day and in our hearts as we toasted him with the last of his favorite whiskey.

- We rode up the mountains on horseback to a place we all used to ride and that he loved deeply. At the falls he often paused at, we let his ashes fly free in the wind. We laughed and swore at him when some blew back on us.

- We had each person stop on the way to the Celebration of Life and pick a wildflower or two. We had several of the beautiful vases and jugs she had made on her potter's wheel, and as people entered, they put their flower in one. We took them to the front to place by her photo. She loved wildflowers, and I hope she forgave us for picking them.

- We had everybody dress in red, as she really didn't like the old tradition of black funerals.

- She had hundreds of books in a dozen or more genres. We took them to the ceremony and had people take at least one on their way out. What was left we donated to the library if they were new and recent, and took the rest to the second-hand store. To her, throwing a book away was a sin.

- At the reception, we put sheets of paper on the table with the following questions: How long did you know Mom? How did you meet her? What's a funny or emotional moment you shared with her? Anything else you want to share for her family's "MOM remembered" notebook? Please include your name and contact. Thank you for taking the time to share. It truly matters.

- She collected angels and had well over five hundred, so we took them all to the funeral and had a big sign at the door asking each person to please collect the angel(s) you gave her. And everyone else please take an angel to live with you in her memory. Even kids were encouraged to take one. (**ME:** You can do the same with Christmas ornaments or any other collection.)
- At his funeral, we watched a video of him singing the song he had written for his wife on their 25th Wedding Anniversary. They were high school sweethearts, and it was the most profound and touching experience you could ever imagine.

* * *

U is for UNUSUAL PLACES TO REMEMBER YOUR LOVED ONE

Me: There are so many places we feel our loved ones after they die. Many people go to the graveside, but I discovered just about everybody has that other special place where they stand or sit and "the feeling" surrounds them. For instance, my wooden angel made from wood scraps from the old house is where I feel Mom and Dad the most.

Me: I go to the garage to commune with my husband. His tools are still there, and he spent a lot of creative time in there. I love touching what he touched. Also, he's got a big presence at the cabin. When I first returned there, I could feel him all around me. I see his beautiful spirit in the sounds and sights of bonfires, water of all kinds, the wind, the rain, falling snow, leaves. There's a strong feeling of him showing me nature with open eyes instead of being closed off by pain.

Ursula: When I go in the barn, every one of my senses is reminded of him. The warm animals, the hay, and yes, even the smell of manure. I listen to the horses eating and nickering, and I hear him soothing them. The sight of his one horse's bright eyes, same beautiful brown as his, looking at me with love. I run my hand down his horse's soft, shiny neck and put my cheek up against it where I can talk and cry. I put on his gloves and run my hand over the wood in the stalls he leaned against and the thick handle of the grain bucket he used. I can taste the dust in the air. I could almost move into the barn. That's where I can always feel his spirit still loving his animals and me.

Other places:

- I'm sure she went to Heaven, because she was one of the best people I've ever known. But I don't know enough about what's up there, so I imagine she's on a cloud of marshmallows. So when I eat marshmallows, or see clouds that look like puffy marshmallows, I see her.
- He rides on my motorbike with me. Sometimes I just sit on it in the driveway so I can feel him with me.
- Anywhere near the river and the lake. He loved it, and when we take his boat out, I feel him riding with us, happy and calming.
- Sitting on the stairs of our church where we met.
- On the wooden swing his dad built for him.
- Among the clothes at a second-hand store, because that's where she got all her clothes, and we always had so much fun shopping together.
- In the passenger seat of my truck. She was such a joy to travel with.
- In a rainstorm or a snowstorm. She always said she was the storm.
- At the opera.
- In the hockey arena.

* * *

Notes

V is for VAGUE

Me: The word vague means not clearly understood, indefinite in nature, character, or form. It explains a lot of what we struggle to hear and see and understand in initial grief.

Vern: Everything seemed so foggy for days after. The report from the police seemed vague, even though everybody else understood it. The doctor's information seemed vague, and she too had told me everything she could. Others understood it. I realized a day or a week after that I had only heard every second or third word, or parts of sentences, and couldn't process what I had been told. I couldn't process what I thought I was hearing and couldn't make decisions because there was no solid thought in my head to hold on to. "Maybe" was a word I used a lot, because I only had a vague understanding of the questions I was being asked. I think my mind was trying to protect me from seeing through that fog too soon.

Valerie: I have a vague recollection of the collision and maybe seeing him dead. I see a part of a blue vehicle. I hear glass shattering. I see blood somewhere. I see the sleeve of his jacket. I see a flash of an EMT. And little snippets of things flit through my head. But I was told it was too frightening and terrible for my brain to take it all in and remember it, so I don't remember. Even after four years, it's still vague, thanks to my brain. And what I did for a while after the collision is very vague. And that seems OK.

* * *

V is for VIEWING

Me: I hadn't planned on a viewing when my husband died, but it turned out OK. I looked at the body that was a semblance of him and realized without a doubt this was just the vessel that carried his tremendous spirit. "And what a vessel it was!" I said out loud. The coffin was the second least expensive on the market (at his previous insistence) because he would be cremated. The top half of the coffin was a removable piece of plywood. Once the immediate family had time alone with him, fourteen of us gathered around the coffin and had a sip of his favorite wine to toast him. At the same time, our grandsons, three, five, and seven, were in a different room with the top from the coffin, drawing and writing messages on it for Papa with a rainbow of brightly colored markers. I told them I had to have a bright color and to write big, because he didn't have his glasses on. I'm sure his spirit was viewing us and smiling.

Vanessa: My sister said my mom looked beautiful at the viewing. They did her hair exactly like she did it. I went out for a breath of fresh air and a cry because she looked nothing like her vibrant self. The funeral home preparation people did the best they could, but she still looked dead and cold.

Vinny: We didn't have a viewing. The doctor said it wasn't wise because of the nature of the horrible death. We had big photos of him alive and well on the table at the funeral. That's how we needed to remember him. But I have to tell the truth, I wanted to see him to say goodbye and deal with the mental fallout. But again, I knew I couldn't take the chance on what I would see and never forget. So I took the doctor's advice and I remember the beautiful person he was. I still don't know if that was the right decision.

Val: I went to the hospital morgue to view my wife. Because of the violent death, the nurses didn't want to open the body bag. The best they could do was let me hug her feet through the bag and then hold on where her hand was. They were very kind and asked me to tell them about her. I think I was still in shock because I talked about her quite a bit and we even laughed. That helped hold good memories in my mind and see her beauty before this.

* * *

V is for VISITORS

Victor: At first I felt so overwhelmed with visitors, it agitated me. I finally was told by a good friend that I had a right to say, "Thanks for stopping by, but I'm just not up to seeing anyone right now." True friends understood.

Val: I loved having visitors, once my friends and family made me realize I didn't have to play hostess. I just lay down on the couch and listened to their voices, as the sound of them comforted me. I can't tell you to this day what they discussed, but I knew they were close by.

Vivian: Visitors brought so much food, I couldn't figure out what to do with it. For the first two weeks, other visitors looked after it for me. We just kept putting it on plates and then putting the extra in freezable containers. Honestly, it was months later I found some of it, and I didn't remember getting it or who had brought it. There were no names left on anything. I appreciated it all very much that somebody had gone to that trouble for us, but I know now when I take food to somebody's house after a death, I put it in a freezer container that is oven safe, mark what it is and how to heat it, and never expect my dish back.

Vance: When somebody came to visit, I had nothing to say, because I didn't know what to say. Sometimes I made small talk about the farm, but mostly I just nodded as they talked and said things like, "Things'll sure be different around here." Everything felt so foreign to me, and so empty, and I didn't know how to express that. My neighbor was uncomfortable when he saw the tears, so he stood to leave, patted me on the shoulder, and said, "You'll get through this." His wife gave him a stern look and said to me, "Just sit quiet with your tea," and immediately starting doing things. Doing dishes, clearing off cupboards, putting away food. I felt relief that I didn't have to say anything and that somebody could just quietly be with me while I tried to figure out what the hell was going on.

Victoria: It sounds strange, but one of the visitors I loved came for only a short time, and she brought bottled water, wet wipes, toilet paper, paper towels, hand lotion, a notebook and pen, and Kleenex *with lotion*. We needed all of that because of the number of people in the house that first week, and I didn't want to go shopping. We had lots of food, but she knew what we needed without asking us.

Vick: When our daughter was in the hospital in Intensive Care, a bunch of her high school friends drove six hours to visit her, and we had to turn them away. I appreciated them coming, but we couldn't let them in. No visitors. And we had no intention of entertaining them. She died four days later. They came to the viewing, so they got to see her.

> *"I'm tired of pretending I'm OK when I'm*
> *not OK." – Margaret Thibault*

> *"As you look around at your wonderful, caring visi-*
> *tors, you realize you cannot buy: friends, happiness,*
> *dreams, time, health, love, hope or life. But as long as*
> *your visitors are your friends, they will bring these valu-*
> *able things back into your house." —Margaret Thibault*

* * *

Notes

W is for WHAT YOU THINK INSIDE

You make it through the many faces, many voices, many touches, many words after the funeral. You were there but sitting on the edge of your chair like a bird waiting to launch itself from a branch. You see people at tables with coffee and open-faced egg salad buns. *Yes, you said after every funeral we attended, that's what you wanted. Ironically, it's the one thing I remember.*

Names are hovering somewhere in the air by the faces, but they're not landing on your tongue. *Thank you for coming. I know I know you, but my brain is dead, so I'll nod and make my lips curl up at the sides.*

You could see people's lips move. Sometimes it sounded like they had only a teeny tiny slit in their vocal cords, and this high-pitched message poked at your ears. You knew it was some form or another of them being sorry for you. Or a voice came to you so soft and whispery you thought maybe you had suddenly gone deaf. *Thank you for coming. My ears are broken. They don't know the road to my brain.*

And then a face would be there, a face you love, and their eyes told you they were on your side, by your side. *Oh, friend, I'm so glad you're here. Please stay with me. I need you. I'm in a terrible fight for my sanity.*

Some people whispered a soft touch on your arm and their fingers felt so good. *I'm real. I must still have a body, even if it's a stranger to me right now.* Other times it felt scrapey and rough, and you wanted to run away. *Thank you for coming. I think you have sandpaper glued to your fingers. Maybe your sharp fingernails are growing backwards on your hands. Go home right now and check.*

Some people tried to take your pain away by showing you what pain they were in. *What the hell?* They squeezed out tears, gnashed their teeth, and told you they'll

168

miss him forever. He was like a brother to them. *He was not. I don't remember him liking you. I'm sure you'll manage once you don't have an audience. I really feel like a bitch. I've got to get out of here.*

You say you're going to the bathroom, and instead you sneak home to the house that looks just like it did a week ago. Except.

His coats are hanging at the entrance, above his work boots and running shoes. *I just bought you a new pair of Nikes. Now what?*

His big easy chair is waiting for you to steal a rest in its nest before he gets home and claims it. His quilt is exactly where he left it across the puffy arm and back, and his slippers are beside it. *I can't steal the comfort of his chair from him; it's not a fun game anymore. I don't want to get fuzzy and warm under the quilt to bug him, and I don't want to hold his slippers ransom until he kisses me hello. I just want to fall on the floor.*

GOD DAMN IT! I WANT HIM!

The new fishing gear he bought two weeks ago is still in the living room. He was going to join his friends for a weekend with his old metal boat they all made fun of. *Will you go without him, guys? Do you want his boat for the laughs? Or the tears? Want his new pole and hooks? I don't. I can't.*

There are the fun photos of the two of you on the wall, and of all the family. *I want to look at HIM as a living, breathing human being, not him as colors on a piece of paper. Somebody asked for copies of photos. Who? The kids and grandkids will know who. They'll also soon realize I snuck away from the funeral. Ran away. Got the fuck out of there. Sorry. They'll all be back in a few minutes and be upset with me coming home on my own. I deserve it. Are they the strong ones now? God, I hope I haven't made them feel that way. I just needed a few minutes of quiet after all that. A few hours. A few years.*

The calendar is full of schedules and dates for the two of you. *Oh look, tonight was supposed to be movie night, not fucking funeral night.*

If you looked right now, his workout equipment would still be waiting for its master to have it do his bidding. *You fucking pieces of shit. I thought you were the great gift that would keep him alive so HE would be the one that had to remember I wanted egg salad on open face buns for MY funeral.*

If you looked right now, his name would still be in the phone book. *Yes, it's old-fashioned, but we still have one, and I feel like tearing the page out and burning it. No, I don't. I want him to stay right there, with a name and a place. Forever.*

Seven days ago, he was. He breathed. He laughed. He kissed me and hugged me. He winked. He snored. His skin was warm. His near-nakedness beside me on the sheets still thrilled me. His body worked magnificently. He thought and talked. Which reminds me …

You pick up the landline and dial his cell phone. His deep beautiful voice answers: "Thanks for calling. If I don't answer, leave a message, or try my home number. I want to talk to you." *Oh, my precious man, I'd give my life for it to be that easy.*

* * *

W is for WHOLE BODY

Me: Grieving is a not only a mental but an entire physical body experience. From your hair hurting to the stumbling of your feet and all points in between, grief has ambushed you physically. At first, the amygdala sent shock signals to the hypothalamus, which in turn sent a signal to the adrenal glands, which sent out an adrenaline rush that flooded the body. Other chemicals released saturate everything, including all the organs, causing bodily changes. Exhaustion is very common.

This is a compilation of physical grief symptoms from many people:

HAIR AND SCALP: My hair hurt. It often felt like somebody was pulling it, and I wanted to shave it off … My scalp was so tender, I could hardly draw a brush over it ... I would poke my painful scalp to remind myself this horror movie was real.

EARS: It was like a radio not quite on a station, so what I heard was full of static ... Voices are not what they should sound like ... I heard people saying something, but it registered slowly, as if it had to come through molasses first, or I just didn't hear ... Voices were too loud or too soft, and sometimes I couldn't tell the difference.

EYES: I couldn't see properly. People looked like they were far away when they were close, and big when they were far away ... Mothers looked like their daughters, and daughters looked like mothers. My eyes couldn't tell ages ... People I had known for years looked different for some reason ... My eyes couldn't focus on any one thing for very long. I was told they darted a lot ... My eyes hurt and felt dry in spite of all the tears.

HEAD AND FACE: I had a constant low-level headache that didn't go away with Tylenol ... I had severe migraines I couldn't get rid of until I threw up ... My face felt like I had sunburn and somebody was pinching my cheeks, my forehead, my jaw ... I felt numb but at the same time could feel that every muscle was very tight, especially my forehead and my cheeks ... My teeth and jaw hurt from clenching my teeth.

NECK AND BACK: When I awoke each morning, my neck felt like I had slept on a crooked bed ... The tension was pulling each muscle until I felt it was rock solid ... There were various pains all through my neck and back. When I stood up, I was like a hunchback for a while ... I felt severe pain going from my back, up through one side or the other of my neck, and I thought it might be a stroke.

SHOULDERS: You know you're not breathing deep enough when your shoulders are hunched up around your ears. You have to listen to the people who remind you to drop your shoulders and breathe as deeply as you can ... My shoulders ached as if I'd been carrying a big load through the night.

ARMS AND HANDS: My hands shook so much, I had trouble holding anything, including a coffee cup ... My hands were clenched tightly all the time, so tightly my nails dug in and even made my palm bleed ... I had no strength in my arms and had trouble lifting things. Even light things seemed too heavy ...

My fingers were like useless sausages ... I kept experiencing spasms in my arms and hands.

HEART: It seemed I could physically feel my heart broken and shattered and falling out of my chest ... My chest seemed to press down on my heart, crushing it ... It would race sometimes, and other times I thought it had stopped ... It pounded really hard in my ears. I could hear the swish of blood all the time... I listened to my own heartbeat and kept wondering if he had felt his heart stop beating ... I was overwhelmed thinking about how my heart was keeping me alive, and how, for her, everything stopped at death ... I could feel shards of broken glass or icicles stabbing my heart.

LUNGS: They didn't work. There was no air in them. They hurt. Or sometimes I knew there was too much air, but I couldn't get it to come out except with a cry or cough or deep sigh ... My lungs forgot to breathe in sometimes ... My problems with poor breathing made me feel dizzy ... My lungs felt squashed.

BELLY AND THROAT: Eating was an issue. First, I couldn't swallow anything. And if I did, my belly didn't want it ... I couldn't stop eating ... My belly always felt empty, and I needed to load it up ... My throat closed at the thought of food. But I could drink some type of smoothies others made for me ... Comfort foods like doughnuts, cake, and bread and honey went down OK. My belly wanted them to help fill the black hole there, but I also wanted to puke, as my digestive system was broken ... One day I'd be constipated, the next day I'd have diarrhea ... My throat didn't want to let me swallow anything for several days.

GENITAL AREA: I wanted to have sex all the time to remind myself I was still alive ... I was told that to have an orgasm would help rid me of toxins that had built up. It's true ... For just a moment, sex gave me a different focus and a moment away from the pain ... I couldn't stand the thought of sex in any form, as it seemed selfish and untimely, and an insult ... I felt guilty being alive and enjoying myself. Couldn't do it... Oh my God. I felt my mother was watching us from above, and I couldn't even begin to think about sex, as we were in her house ... Sex can bring you closer together ... Our differences in desire was a real issue.

HIPS: They ached a lot, maybe from sitting, maybe from poor posture, maybe from the way I slept ... It seemed they ached because everything was out of alignment and my whole body ached.

LEGS AND FEET: Everything was off kilter. My legs didn't respond right when I stood up, and I had very little strength in them ... My feet hurt all the time, and I couldn't walk far before I had to sit down ... I tripped a lot and stumbled no matter what I was walking on, and I felt my equilibrium was totally off ... I had agitation and spasms in my legs when I'd lie down to sleep ... I sat a lot, which didn't help my deteriorating muscle tone. I wanted my legs to go exercise themselves while I sought refuge under my quilt.

KNEES: My knees hurt all the time. I couldn't kneel or bend down to get something, because I couldn't get up without a struggle. That was very unusual for me ... At night I couldn't get my knees to bend properly where I could get comfortable ... I slept with a pillow under my knees for months after he died. I had never done that before.

SKIN: It felt like my skin was craving touch, but at the same time was very sensitive ... I didn't want to be touched at all. Other hands felt like sandpaper ... Touch on my skin was what reminded me I was still alive ... My skin felt rough and dry, and I had to keep putting lotion on it ... There was an oddity about my skin. It felt like a new skin that crawled with little buggy things and hurt to the touch ... Sometimes I would pinch the soft skin on my underarm, hoping to wake up from this nightmare ... I had night sweats for a long time ... I would stare at my skin and try to imagine what her soft skin was doing in death. Weird, eh?

BRAIN: My brain was broken. It didn't work as it did before, or as I wanted it to now ... It felt like something was dislodged in my brain ... I was scared, as my brain was sluggish, foggy, overwhelmed, and not doing its job well at all ... I'm a nurse, and it felt like everything needed to be "re-built," including my brain, its many parts, and the chemical disruptions ... My concentration was screwed ... I couldn't process anything for quite a while ... I felt like a zombie whose brain has been sucked away. My brain was still there, but it took its own sweet time to function again, even to a small degree. The zombie feeling finally went away ... I think I would describe it as a struggle to put any thoughts together to try and understand anything ... I was constantly too tired to even think properly.

BLOOD: My blood felt like hot lava going through my body ... My blood felt like ice, like it was frozen in one spot and not moving ... My blood rushed to my ears and kept making a loud noise ... My blood didn't go to my brain, and I fainted ... It seemed like my blood stopped going to my fingers and toes for a few days, and they were always cold

There is a loss of elasticity in brain and body. No snap-
ping back to original abilities. - unknown

The brain weighs three pounds, and consumes 20 percent of
our energy. Can it bring structure to chaos? The amygdala
controls all reactions; controls all emotions, determines
how we will react to fear and trauma. Your brain tries to
help you assemble thoughts into some semblance of nor-
malcy. It's trying to adjust with all this new trauma.

"The instant of great disaster, it is often said, is an
elongated one, as if in witnessing its own demise, the
human mind is wont to wind the moment out long and
then longer still." —Tiffany Baker, Mercy Snow

We can never listen to each other's heartbeats again.

* * *

W is for WILLS

Me: Get a f***ing will done! Don't put it off. Even with a will, you have probably experienced the piles of paperwork that need to be done, and for which you need a Certificate of Death and copy of the will. Otherwise, it goes to Probate and sorting things out is delayed, sometimes for years. Get through your paperwork and then vow not to leave a guess-mess for the next Executor or family member.

- Talk to your lawyer, your accountant, and the funeral director. What needs to be in the will? Who has signing authority on bank accounts and investments of any kind? Who owns what, including the house, vehicles, property, anything else of value? Who initially pays the bills? Who pays the $15,000 or more for the funeral? Who pays the mortgage and car payment? What if his accounts are frozen, which is common after death? Do you have a Living Will with Goals of Care, or a Personal Directive through the Health Department, or at the very least, have you put down your wishes for what happens at certain levels of disability? Is there a donor card or donor wishes?
- If it seems overwhelming to sort your matters out while you're alive, think of how difficult it will be for others to make decisions under their mind-numbing pressure of grief. You have to have a conversation about death long before it happens. Get a f* * *ing will done! AND put your wishes on paper.
- Talk to a lawyer today!
- Talk to your banker or accountant about investments if you have any.
- Contact your provincial government human services office for a Personal Directives Information Kit.

Walter: My wife didn't think she needed a will, as she only owned a few things. A car. A piano. Some clothes. And her name was on everything else jointly with me. So she assumed it would magically revert to me. Ha. Do you know the paperwork that's involved? And do you know how many departments and businesses ask for the will as well as the Death Certificate? And now the family is fighting over who gets the piano, her pension, the car, the jewelry (which it turns out she had quite a bit of), and anything else they think might be worth anything. They even argued about whether she should be cremated or not. Jesus. It's a bad time to find out you have no will to refer to and you've raised two very selfish girls.

Winnie: It was easy to get a simple will done, as you can get the forms off the Internet. That's as long as things are crystal clear in your situation. I started with that but then went to a lawyer to ensure everything was written down the way it should be with our investments. You don't realize how complicated things can be when you're trying to be fair to everyone.

* * *

Notes

X is the FIRST UNKNOWN

Me: X is the first unknown quantity in algebra. There's a formula, but everything is unknown until you get more information and start solving it. There is no formula for accepting death or for grieving, but every step of the way you're looking for more information, trying to solve what the unknown means, and what the next step might then be. You will get there.

*   *   *

Notes

Y

is for YEARNING

Me: There will come a point in your grief where the yearning for your loved one and the life you had becomes overwhelming. Just when you think you're coping somewhat better, this overwhelming persistent longing for your loved one debilitates you. Again you may feel you're losing your mind, but I assure you this is an identifiable pain on the grief journey. It steals days or maybe weeks from you, and there's an incredible pain while it's happening, but it will pass eventually.

Yolanda: I thought I was doing OK, until one night I woke up in the middle of the night with a gut-wrenching yearning for him. I made it worse by touching his pillow and his cold side of the bed. But it wasn't just that. It was all-consuming, and I couldn't get out of bed the next morning. Or the next, or the next. I cried through it all. But I did get up. And I went to sleep in the twin bed in the guest room until I could handle the yearning and the aloneness. And now I'm back in our big bed.

Yettie: I was trudging through the quicksand wondering what was next. And it was the terrible yearning, the deep longing to have him back. I hoped he was just gone on a business trip and would be back soon, maybe tomorrow. But I knew it was bullshit, and after I hurt and cried for days, I finally realized this was now the rest of my life without him.

Me: You want him. You need her. You can't function without him. It's suddenly difficult to breathe without her. Your unmerciful desire to have him back cuts very deep. Just when you thought you had your anxiety pretty well under control, your yearning brought it back. The yearning is so strong you feel like you can touch it. But it's an abstract leaving concrete hurts in its wake. So you can't catch it and throw it out. You can only recognize it for what it is—a part of the process.

Look at photos. Cry. Remember good stuff. Cry. Talk. Cry. Holler. Pound your pillow. I swear it will eventually be under control, with your intentional work.

* * *

Y is for YESTERDAY

Me: I know why life doesn't let us foresee the future: because we would never let go of yesterday if we knew it was the last day with someone we loved. Yesterday everything was OK. Everybody wants yesterday back, before the death. No matter what happened in yesterday's twenty-four hours, compared to today, it was simple and good. In most cases, nobody knew the next day would become a "death date."

Yesterday we were totally different people with a totally different life. But the more yesterdays we can say we got through, the more it means we are moving on. Yesterday is gone. So what can we do with the twenty-four hours of today? If you just want to cry all day, that's OK. If you just want to breathe as deeply as you can, that's good too. The sun will still rise and set. Tomorrow will come anyway, and today will be yesterday.

Notes

Z is for 'ZACTLY

Me: When our four RCMP officers were shot and killed in Mayerthorpe on March 3, 2005, people from all over the world sent notes, cards, emails, letters, poetry, and other items of condolence.

School teachers from across Canada, bless their hearts, took time with their students to help them deal with their fears and sadness. If a bad man could kill four police officers, then am I safe? Depending on their ages, they wrote letters, drew, colored, wrote poetry, made posters, made banners, and sent big hearts of love. Those children can't imagine how much their offerings meant to those they sent them to.

Several older students wrote that they wanted to join the police force to "kill the bad guy before he could kill me." They all did whatever they could to try to understand and digest what this terrible historical tragedy meant to them.

But the one message that sticks in my heart still, all these years later is a Grade 2 girl who wrote: "I know 'zactly how you feel. My rabbit died." I think of her often and find myself saying, "That's 'zactly how I feel." Bless her sweet heart. May that be the most difficult thing for her to grieve for a long time.

* * *

Z is for ZEN

"You either get bitter or you get better. It's that simple. You either take what has been dealt to you and allow it to make you a better person, or you allow it to tear you down. The choice does not belong to fate. It belongs to you." —Zen Conscious, <u>Portapique</u>

* * *

Z is for ZIGZAG THOUGHTS

Me: I honestly didn't know where else to put this information, so it's in Zigzag. Because it can either be funny or sad, depending on your mood. There are always odd or bizarre stories from others that just ricochet around in your mind like a bag of spilled marbles.

• An aunt at Grandad's funeral started her own unscheduled eulogy, asking the crowd to sing "Happy Birthday" to her, as that day was actually her birthday. She then started a speech to tell how Grandpa had wronged her. We hadn't seen her for years and didn't realize how far downhill she had gone mentally. We were all shocked, and it took my brother a minute to get up there and thank her and take her back to her seat. We could handle the Happy Birthday song, but not her words after. We should have been better prepared.

• A friend's son walking down the aisle with his mother's ashes stopped, looked at his grandma, who was already seated on the left side, and said, "Bitch." Then set the urn down on the table and went to sit on the right side. He gave a eulogy as if nothing had happened. I knew my friend had put up with a lot of nastiness from her mother-in-law, but the son's actions were so quick it was almost like it didn't happen. And many people at the luncheon after agreed. Grandma really was a bitch.

- Friends of ours in another province wrote their own obituaries with the help of each other and their kids. Then they built two plain bookshelves and called them future coffins. They also prepaid their funerals and said they are reminded every day that death makes life worth living to the fullest, and that love should rule the day, every day. What a beautiful gift to give each other.

- A friend said you die three times. Once physically, wherever that may be. Once at the viewing as many people who know you gaze upon you for the last time, or later at the funeral when they realize you're actually dead. And once when there's no one still alive who actually knew you.

- I asked the middle-aged man in the viewing area at the medical examiner's office what his most memorable situation was. He said a lovely little gray-haired lady with a cane limped in and leaned against the viewing window. She asked if "he" was really dead. The worker said "Yes" and asked if she needed help. She turned to him with a smile and said, "No thank you. I just had to make sure the old son of a bitch was really dead. Thank you." And out she limped.

- A woman whose eighty-six-year-old brother had died a month before showed up at a Fiftieth Anniversary party and said, "We were going to stay home, but we came because they came to our fiftieth a few years ago. But we decided we're not going to have a good time. It wouldn't be right." WHAAAAT?

- My sister and I snuck a note into our dad's coffin. When we were kids, our dog died. We weren't sure what death was, so we hung around Rusty waiting for him to jump up and play. Mom insisted we bury him rather than leave him out to look at. Dad's words before we covered Rusty were: "Ashes to ashes, dust to dust. We didn't want to bury you, but Mom says we must." He laughed and laughed. Guess what note we put in Dad's coffin? We laughed until we cried. And cried. And cried.

- My uncle had had too much to drink, but we went to the liquor store for more anyway. We told the snooty cashier we were at our family home for our other uncle's funeral. Without a word of warmth, she said "Oh, did he finally die?" And without missing a beat, my tipsy uncle looked into her cranky face and said, "No. We're just practicing."

A *closing message from ME:*

Thank you for trusting there would be something in this book for you. I remind you that you are not alone and that you are not losing your mind. You can and will survive what has become the most brutal of all times in your life. Be kind to yourself and take all the time you need as you move from the person you were to the person you are today, this minute. You are the best you can be, on your way to even better.

My wish for you is this: With time and intent you will move from **victim** to **survivor** to **prevailer.**

As **victim** you are the one that was stabbed in the heart as the result of a death, and for a while you feel helpless and lost.

As **survivor**, you breathe better and are coping with life a lot better. You lived through the worst of the pain, and you are learning to live in a new world.

But as **prevailer**, you rise above the pain of grief, find your energy and focus, and do something positive with your situation. It doesn't have to be big (e.g., a scrapbook, a poem, a trip), but it has to give you a sense of victory.

> *"The reality is that you will grieve forever. You will not 'get over' the loss of a loved one; you will learn to live with it. You will heal and you will rebuild yourself around the loss you have suffered. You will be whole again but you will never be the same. Nor should you be the same nor would you want to."—Elisabeth Kubler-Ross*

Heaven's Veil

by Margaret Thibault, for Frank Thibault, who was killed at the age of 69 on April 14, 2019

I am here and you are there, now separated by Heaven's veil,
As I see you sitting on your cloud, I'm stumbling along life's trail.
We thought we had forever when we said "Til death do us part."
As I slipped the ring on your finger, I also gave you my heart.
For all those years together, we shared our hopes, plans, and dreams,
And our love was so deep and contented, such a precious gift it seemed.
But life has the ultimate power, it works in its unexpected way,
And the heart I so loved forever stopped beating one tragic day.
Now you're not by my side where I need you, and all alone I fear,
Moving on with the life we treasured, on a difficult road it's clear.
But I can't live small when we loved so big, hand in hand when life was kind.
You left behind special memories in the house I've built in my mind.
So I am here knowing you are there, and I remember each special detail.
I will love you forever with all my heart, until I meet you beyond Heaven's veil.

Love and Hugs to all the broken hearts—MARGARET

Printed in Canada